THE JIMMY INGLE STORY

With an
introduction by
PATRICK MYLER

BRANDON

First published in Ireland 1984
Brandon Book Publishers Ltd
Cooleen, Dingle, Co. Kerry.

First published in the United States of America 1984
Brandon Book Publishers Ltd
51 Washington Street
Dover, New Hampshire 03820.

British Library Cataloguing in Publication Data
Ingle, Jimmy
    The Jimmy Ingle Story.
    I. Ingle, Jimmy 2. Boxers (Sports) —
    Ireland — Biography
    I. Title
    796.8'3'0924 GV1132.13/

ISBN 0-86323-073-8

Cover design: Syd Bluett and Steve MacDonogh
Typesetting: Leaders Phototypesetting, Swords, Ireland
Printed at Lucan, Co. Dublin, Ireland by Colourgraphics Ltd.

Contents

Illustrations

Jimmy Ingle in 1983.

Introduction

The famous St. Andrew's Amateur Boxing Club had its headquarters at the rear of a decaying tenement house in York
Street, Dublin. To gain access to the gymnasium you had to
go through the aptly-named Glover's Alley, a narrow cobble-
stoned laneway running alongside the Royal College of
Surgeons on the west side of St. Stephen's Green. Like so
many once elegant townhouses of the Georgian aristocracy,
Number 42 York Street is no longer with us. When the bull-
dozers moved in they took St. Andrews with them to oblivion.
What the planners and developers like to call progress may
have wiped away the edifice, but it has not erased the memory
of a fight factory that produced a constant supply of great
amateur ringmen during its heyday of the thirties and forties.
Legendary names like Mattie Rodgers, Ernie Smith, winner of
eight Irish senior championships, Jack Foley, Paddy Byrne,
Tommy Byrne, Jack Kennedy, Paddy Gernon, Christy Forde,
Al McDermott, Peter Foran, and the fantastic Ollie Byrne
whose career spanned thrity-six years and who was in his
fiftieth year when he hung up his gloves. Oh yes, and Jimmy
Ingle . . .

Jimmy had long since discarded his amateur vest for the
more demanding, but more lucrative, pastures of the professional ring when I, as a hesitant twelve-year-old, was per-
suaded by a pal to go along with him and join St. Andrew's.

His father took us down to the club one Sunday morning after mass. My introduction to the strange world of the boxing breed was at once an exhilarating and an intimidating experience. Merely to be in the presence of instantly recognisable stars of National Stadium fight nights was a great thrill, but it was tempered somewhat by the claustrophobic atmosphere of the place. The stale air was filled with nauseous smells of leather and sweat and little clouds of dust were churned up every time a skipping rope hit the bare boards or nimble feet danced this way and that. I was later to learn that boxing gymnasia are the same all over the world. It was Gene Tunney, the retired undefeated world heavyweight champion, who once, while training at the Stillman's Gym on New York's Eighth Avenue, complained about the lack of fresh air, only to hear a fellow world champion, featherweight Johnny Dundee, retort, "Fresh air? Why, that stuff is likely to kill us."

The distinctive noises of the gymnasium are something else that sticks in the memory. The rhythmic beat of the rope-skippers, the snorts and grunts as grim-faced boxers threw hooks and uppercuts at shadows that weren't there, the dull thud of the heavy bag as others dug vicious punches into an imaginary opponent's solar plexus, the hypnotic drumbeat of the small ball as it swivelled crazily on its mooring as its attacker sharpened his reflexes with precise blows, the groans from the floor area as men twisted themselves into unbelievable contortions in the name of exercise, the rasping bark of the trainer as he urged greater effort out of unwilling sparrers in the ring. It is a cacophony as familiar to gym users everywhere as the language of animals is to the jungle dweller.

My pal and I paid our one and sixpence to join St. Andrew's, which entitled us to train there three nights a week as well as on Sunday. mornings. Unlike Jimmy Ingle and others, my appearance on the boxing scene caused no great stir. There was no sudden hush, no breaking-off of activity around the gym when I climbed between the ropes, such as there was when one of the club's star performers went a couple of rounds with a seasoned sparring partner. Along with the other nonentities I went through the motions of practising the straight left and the right cross in front of a mirror and tried manfully, if in vain, to master the technique of jumping at the same time as the skipping rope reached the floor.

There was one brief moment during my unspectacular stint at St. Andrew's when the trainer did notice that I wasn't part of the sparse gym furniture – and it involved an Ingle. Not Jimmy, of course, but his younger brother Ignatius, who went by the name of Nago. I suppose shouts of "Come on, Ignatius" wouldn't go down too well with the hardened fight crowds. Nago was one of nine Ingle brothers, all of whom were boxers. He was a promising junior boxer and a class above the general mediocrity, which included yours truly, at St. Andrew's. One evening he found himself short of a sparmate and, in desperation, his gaze settled on me, still trying to untangle my skinny legs from that skipping rope. "Hey, how'd you like to go a few rounds with me?" he called. I shrugged my shoulders resignedly, just as a condemned man would if asked if he would like to test the rope that was to be used to hang him.

The very name of Ingle struck abject fear into my bones. Even if he had only been a second cousin of a second cousin, but was still called Ingle, the effect would have been the same. My feet seemed rivetted to the floor as another youngster encased my puny fists in the huge sixteen-ounce gloves that were used in training. They were known in the fight trade as "pillows". The title seemed appropriate, for I was convinced I would be resting my head on them as I reclined on the canvas in about ten seconds. A small group of boxers gathered by the side of the ring, maintaining the pretence of training by jogging up and down or whipping a fist into an open hand, something akin to the old French hags who clicked away with their knitting needles as they watched the drop of the guillotine. There was an audible sigh of disappointment, I thought, when the trainer gave me a reprieve. He had been out of the gym for a few minutes and returned just as I was about to duck between the ropes. "No, you can't go in with Ingle, you're not ready for him yet," he called. I muttered a silent prayer of thanksgiving to St. Jude as I pulled off the "pillows" and went back to sparring in front of the mirror. Reflections don't hit back.

St. Andrew's, sadly, was no longer a strong force in amateur boxing then, in the early fifties, and its more ambitious members drifted off to other clubs throughout the city where they could be guaranteed more regular activity and encouragement. The older men who hung around the York Street premises regretted the club's decline and spoke about the great days when St. Andrew's really meant something on a boxing bill. They talked especially about the greatest day in its history, 22 April 1939, when a lanky seventeen-year-old Jimmy Ingle made boxing history by becoming the first Irishman to win a European championship. What an occasion of joy that must have been, not only for St. Andrew's or even for Irish amateur boxing, but for the country at large. With Europe on the brink of being plunged into armed conflict, there was much despair about and anything that relieved the mood of despondency, however fleeting, was heartily welcomed. The boxing championships were not without the taint of political partisanship, with some of the ringside judges being more influenced by what country a boxer came from than what he did inside the ropes. Blatantly bad decisions were rife, but fortunately the Juré d'Appel had the power to reverse unfair verdicts. Jimmy Ingle was almost robbed of his moment of glory when he was adjudged to have lost his semi-final bout against an Italian. However, justice was done when the decision was reversed and the young Dubliner went on to win the European flyweight title. His success served to inspire another Irish contestant, Paddy Dowdall, who captured the featherweight honour that same night. A measure of the Irish boys' achievement is that in the forty-five years since then only two other Irishmen (Gerry O'Colmain in 1947 and Maxie McCullagh in 1949) have managed to emulate their feat.

It was shortly afterwards, on a trip to the United States with an Irish team, that Ingle made such a favourable impression on Gene Tunney that the ex-world heavyweight champion offered to manage him if he would turn professional and stay in America. Jimmy, an honourable man, declined as he had already given his word to the well-known English boxing manager Ted Broadribb that he would let him do the job. As fate had it, neither Tunney nor Broadribb became his manager, but his long-time friend and amateur trainer David Stewart.

It it interesting to speculate on how much he might have achieved had he gone with Tunney or Broadribb. New York-born Tunney, whose parents were emigrants from Kiltimagh, Co. Mayo, was one of the most respected figures in boxing. A master boxer, he had won the world title from the great Jack Dempsey and survived the famous "long count" to retain the crown in a return match, then retired unbeaten champion and a self-made millionaire. With his expertise in ring technique and his wide connections, who knows what he might have managed in guiding the dedicated young Dubliner? As for Broadribb, it is perhaps just as well that the war halted the proposed liaison between Ingle and himself. The Englishman, although he took Welshman Tommy Farr to a world heavyweight title crack at Joe Louis and was the man behind Freddie Mills's world light-heavyweight title success, leaves some large question marks over the way he steered Mills's career. Any boxing manager who could see his man take the sort of punishment that Mills took from world champion Gus Lesnevich in their first fight, when he was knocked out in ten rounds, then let him take on the British heavyweight champion Bruce Woodcock three weeks later to suffer another defeat, and later the same year watch him take a pitiful hiding from the American heavyweight Joe Baksi, must have been more preoccupied with the financial rewards than his man's physical welfare.

Certainly Ingle would have made more money from boxing had he spent his prime years in England or in the United

States. The biggest purse of his career was the £200 he received for taking on a young Randolph Turpin at Coventry in 1947. He earned every penny, for he took an unmerciful pounding from the tigerish "Leamington Licker", then en route to the British and world middleweight titles. For his professional debut five years earlier at the Rotunda Cinema in Dublin Jimmy received the princely sum of £25. It may seem poor compensation now, but it represented the equivalent of ten weeks' wages at his job as a sawyer at the time. Professional boxing, except for those at the very top, pays only supplementary benefits. It is a precarious way of trying to make a full-time living. An interesting revelation by Jimmy is that he received £10 for his last "amateur" fight. The payment was made by an official of the Corinthians Amateur Boxing Club. Later Ingle discovered that his opponent, Spike McCormack, a member of the promoting club, had been given £30 for his efforts. Shamateurism, obviously, is nothing new in Irish sport.

By his own admission, Ingle probably left it too late in turning professional. The time to make the change was after winning the European amateur championship, while he was still in his late teens. He had already had over a hundred contests by the time he turned to the paid ranks and he had grown into a welterwieght, subsequently moving up to middleweight. He was rather too short in height and reach to match many of his contemporaries. Nevertheless, he suffered only seven setbacks in thirty-nine professional contests up to the end of the war, so he gave quite a creditable account of himself in domestic encounters with an impressive line-up of talent in the thriving middleweight division.

It wasn't until 1946 that Ingle got the chance to show his worth in opposition to the reigning British welterweight and middleweight champion Ernie Roderick. The referee's decision was a draw, but almost everyone else in the packed Theatre Royal, Dublin, thought the Irishman should have won. Jimmy failed narrowly to beat two other holders of the British middleweight crown, Vince Hawkins and Albert Finch, and he was way past the time when he should have hung up the gloves when he lost to Finch in a return match. A first round defeat by Alex Buxton, who later won the British light-heavyweight title, finally convinced the brave Dubliner to call it quits in 1950. After eighteen hard years campaigning as an amateur and a professional, he had earned his retirement.

Had he been boxing today, he would undoubtedly have applied to become a British citizen in order to qualify for a British title fight, as did Mick Leahy and Spike McCormack's two sons, "Young" John and Pat, among others, in more recent years. Such a move would not have been considered prudent during the later forties, when Irish people were more strongly nationalistic and would probably have condemned such action as treasonable. Nor would Britain have taken too kindly to such an appeal from a citizen of a nation which adopted a neutral stance for the duration of the Second World War. Had circumstances been different, there is every reason to believe that Ingle, with the inspiration of a British title at stake and the stepping stone to greater success that that could provide, might well have become the first Southern Irishman to take home a Lonsdale Belt.

Happily, his long service to the toughest of all sports has left no permanent marks on Jimmy Ingle. He retains his devotion to the game and is as popular and as widely respected by boxing folk everywhere as he is with the citizens of his adopted home town of Luton in Bedfordshire. Indeed, one can only marvel at the sharpness of his brain in recalling even minor details of people, places and events going back to his childhood up to sixty years ago. His autobiography is more than a story of boxing and boxers, it is an evocation of a Dublin that is, sadly, no longer with us. A Dublin when times were tougher but when honesty and integrity stood for something. A Dublin of tramcars, of pitch-and-toss schools, of bringing home turf from the mountains for the fire, of Gardai who would chase you for kicking a ball in the streets, clip you around the ear and tell you to get off home. A Dublin of great characters like Johnny Fortycoats, Bang Bang, Alfie Byrne, Cyclone Billy Warren and Hector Grey, the latter now the sole survivor.

For me, it is an honour and a privilege to have been asked to write this introduction to Jimmy Ingle's book. I have long admired him from a distance and I am glad to have been given the opportunity of paying him this small tribute. On top of the many honours he earned in the ring, we now have Jimmy Ingle, author. Chalk it up as another winning debut.

Patrick Myler
Dublin
July 1984

Preface

When I started my boxing career in January 1932 I was a tiny ten-year old schoolboy weighing five stone. I little dreamed then that some fifty years later old boxing magazines, newspaper cuttings and my scrapbooks would be of such help in enabling me to write my autobiography.

Many former boxing champions have had their autobiographies written for them by ghost writers. But Gene Tunney wrote *A Man Must Fight* himself, and for me it ranks as the finest of autobiographies. Of course, he was a very articulate man and even in his boxing days corresponded regularly with Bernard Shaw. I am no Gene Tunney but, like him, I have written this book my way.

* * * * * *

I would like to acknowledge with gratitude the assistance given me by so many boxing enthusiasts: Harry Mullan and Ron Oliver of *Boxing News;* John O'Donnell, Jim McDonald, Willie Clarke and Vic Hardwicke — record compilers extraordinary — who helped with details of my professional career; the late Arthur MacWeeney, Peter Wilson, Dick Wilkes, Arthur McGahan, W. Buchan Taylor, Thomas Myler, Mitchel Cogley and James Butler. Both the *Irish Post* and Colm Ó Torna played a big part in having my story published. I would also like to thank my brother John; my Dad, whose introduction to Paddy Fagan initiated a family tradition which led to our being described in the newspapers as "the fighting Ingles"; the boxers and officials of the amateur and professional associations; and my late manager and trainer David Stewart, who made it all possible.

Jimmy Ingle
Luton
July 1984

Jimmy Ingle in 1937, at the age of fifteen, after he had won the 6 stone 7 pounds juvenile championship of Ireland.

1. Dublin in the rare ould times

Cleaning the attic recently, I came on a framed certificate covered in dust, with its glass shattered. But the parchment was intact. It proclaimed that in 1937 I became the six stone, seven pounds juvenile boxing champion of all Ireland. Memories came flooding back – of my childhood and schooldays in Dublin and the start of my boxing career in January 1932. How the years have flown!

We lived in Dublin's Ringsend in Penrose Street which was directly opposite Shelbourne Park, then the home ground of the famous Shelbourne soccer club. I was born on 21 July 1921 and delivered by the local midwife, Nurse Byrne of Hastings Street. I weighed in at only five pounds.

My granny Ingle sublet the top room to my parents for four shillings a week (20p) and she paid the landlord, Mr. Brass, eight shillings a week rent for the house.

I was baptised in Ringsend Catholic Church and, in deference to both my grandfathers, was christened James John.

When I was three years old I contracted scarlet fever, chicken pox and measles. Dr. Westtrop, our local physician, was sent for and he arrived on his bicycle. After examining me, he told my parents I had a contagious disease and would have to go to an isolation hospital. The ambulance duly came. It was a horse-drawn square box on wheels; there was a door at the rear and a tiny window on the side. Two men in peaked caps, and with coats almost reaching their ankles, carried me down the narrow stairs in a blanket. Then one of them drove the horse while the other sat inside with me. When we arrived at our destination – Clonskea Fever Hospital – I was placed in a small room. I don't remember much more but my dad told me afterwards that I lapsed into a coma and was unconscious for a few days. Apparently, I nearly died but somebody was praying for me and, in due course, I made a good recovery. The same ambulance and men eventually returned me home to my relieved parents.

Our house was very small – two up and two down. There was no kitchen, just a scullery measuring about six feet by three feet, containing an iron gas cooker which was the property of the Dublin Alliance Gas Company and a glazed sink with a cold-water tap. There was an outside lavatory at the end of a small, concreted yard. To keep warm during the winter months, we huddled over an open coal fire. Our only lighting was from an oil lamp which was on the mantelpiece above the fireplace.

By the time I was five years old I had three brothers – John, Charles and Joseph. Three of us slept in a brass double bed in the back room which we shared with our grandfather. He slept in an iron single bed on the other side of the room.

A major event of those childhood years was the resurfacing of the street. Piles of stone chippings were shovelled on to boiling tar discharged from a huge boiler. Then along came the steamroller to flatten it all. Parents on the street asked the men's permission to allow those of their children who had colds to come close and breathe the fumes of the foaming tar.

Dublin was full of characters in those days and some, such as Johnny Forty Coats, are still remembered. Johnny was a frequent sight on our street. Whether in winter or summer, he was attired in a succession of ragged coats. He wore a greasy battered hat and there was a cigarette permanently between his lips. He always wore slippers with socks pulled over the trousers legs. His grey beard was long and matted. Tin cans hung from his belt and he begged for pennies.

17

Another great character of my childhood was "Battery" Austin. He was the "boxman" at the pitch-and-toss school in the narrow lanes at the back of the houses. He sorted out the bets when the halfpennies hit the ground. His word was law. Dissent meant getting a battering – hence his name. He was over six feet tall and built in proportion. He kept order. The pitch-and-toss school was frequently harrassed by two Gardai who were nicknamed "Lousy Shoulders" and "Hot Potato". When they raided, everybody scattered – usually by climbing over walls. Normally, the neighbours were only too happy to help people escape by letting them run through the house.

My dad and grandad were dock labourers who worked for the Merchant Warehousing Company unloading grain ships. They carried sacks, each of which weighed 16 stone. A plank stretched from the ship to the quayside and the men walked that plank with their load. The sacks were put on horse-drawn drays which, when loaded, were galloped to the granaries. The men worked from six o'clock in the morning to six in the evening. There was a half-hour dinner break. They were paid ten old pennies an hour.

Dad's name was Charlie, but he was nicknamed "Hoppy" as his right leg was an inch shorter than his left. He limped badly. As a boy of twelve years, he had contracted rheumatism. There were no pain-killing drugs in those years of my childhood. Most days, Dad arrived home from work in agony. I remember my mother massaging his legs with Sloan's Liniment to relieve the pain. Dad was a keen pigeon fancier and for many years held the record of winning twelve consecutive races. He excelled also at pigeon shows, often winning the award for the best bird in the competition. But his happiness was not infrequently marred when a cat invaded the loft. The mutilated pigeons had to be destroyed.

School began for me in September 1926. My mam bought me hob-nailed boots, corduroy trousers and a gansey (pullover) in Kitty Whelan's drapery store in Thorncastle Street, Ringsend. These items were purchased on the "never-never" system, but my mother was a reliable customer and paid off regularly. I held my mother's hand as I walked to school for the first time, gazing in wonder at the huge gasometers towering over South Lots Road. We passed under the railway bridge at Bath Avenue and I saw the magnificent steam trains overhead. Then we went into St. Mary's Church, Haddington Road and said a few prayers. Soon I was sitting at a desk for the first time and the nuns were teaching us the alphabet.

It didn't take me too long to learn to read and write. Next came the purchase of my first comic which, having read every word, I swapped with my two school chums, Paddy Hyland and Oliver Curley.

I made my First Communion in May 1928, when I was nearly seven years old. My aunt Bridget, Mam's youngest sister, brought me to Clery's department store in O'Connell Street where I was fitted out with a black velvet suit, white silk shirt and patent leather shoes. I was her godchild and nothing but the best would do. Bridget was a maid working in a big house in Seaford Terrace, Sandymount. She was paid five shillings (25p) a week. From this sum, she had saved to make sure that I was well attired for this great day in my young life.

On a wet and windy Sunday morning in January 1932, I joined St. Joseph's Boxing Club. The No. 3 tram at Ringsend Road was full and, by the time the next one arrived, I was soaking wet. The conductor, seeing my bedraggled appearance, didn't ask me to pay the penny fare to my destination – Westland Row. I remember noticing that, outside Westland Row railway station, there were clouds of steam rising from the jarvies' horses as they stood there soaking wet. The jarvies themselves were sheltering in the public lavatory, awaiting passengers from the trains requiring their services. I walked down Lombard Street, crossed over Townsend Street into Moss Street and a few minutes later reached St. Joseph's Boxing Club. It was a former football club premises and was quite large. A hot, wood-burning stove was a welcome sight. I removed my wet clothes and changed into shorts, singlet and plimsoles. Mr. Fagan was in charge. He was a former professional fighter. He laced a pair of boxing gloves on my small hands and gave me my first boxing lesson. There were a few onlookers who smoked and, once in a while, spat on the glowing stove which then sizzled. They seemed to approve of my beginner's efforts.

In those days, the Irish army's Portobello Barracks was the venue for all the major amateur boxing occasions, both national championships and internationals. The National Stadium wasn't built until 1939. My dad brought me along to see the national championship in March 1932. It was a magical night for me. The champions to emerge that night were: fly, Frankie Kerr (Arbour Hill); bantam, Paddy Hughes (Corinthians); feather, Ernie Smith (St. Andrew's); light, Jack Kennedy (St. Andrew's); welter, Larry Flood (Army); middle, Jack Chase (Garda); light-heavy, Willie Murphy (Garda); heavy, Jim Mulligan (Garda). Some of those men were legends in Irish amateur boxing and their names are still recalled with reverence by all who followed the sport.

The juvenile championships were held at Portobello Barracks the following month and, although I was new to the sport, I was entered. The weigh-in was at Elvery's, The Elephant House in O'Connell Street. The late J. J. Healy was clerk of the scales and he smilingly told me I was five stone. I was drawn against Jack Harte (now a senator) from the Corinthian Club.

As we entered the barrcks that evening, there was a sinking feeling in my tummy. The sentry smiled at our tiny figures. He had, of course, seen it all before and, no doubt, would see it frequently again in the years to come, but for me it was a momentous occasion. I beat John Harte on points. Afterwards he shook my hand and wished me well in my next bout with Brendan Kelly from St.Andrew's Club. Brendan was already an Irish juvenile champion and easily beat me on points.

But that was nothing in comparison to the following Monday at School. The teacher, Mr. Black, had me up at the blackboard to answer some questions on a plan he had drawn of the classroom. Every mistake I made resulted in a vicious stroke of the cane over the exposed flesh between my short trousers and stockings. To try and minimise the agony, I put my hands at the back of my legs and soon my fingers were lacerated. If I have ever hated anyone, I hated Mr. Black that day. At the lunchbreak, I slipped through the school gates and went home. My mother reacted: "Jesus, Mary and Holy Saint Joseph, what's happened to you?" When I told her, she responded: "May God forgive him." My fingers were by now badly swollen and the back of my legs covered in weals. Dad took me to school the next morning and asked Mr. Black why he had inflicted such injury on a small boy. He told the teacher that if it ever happened again he would return to the school and punch his head off. Mr. Black apologised and said he had not meant to hurt me. He gave my father an assurance that it wouldn't happen again. A few weeks later, Mr. Black was involved in an accident on his motorcycle. He was badly injured and died soon afterwards.

I beat a lad named Duffy in June of that year at Donnolly's Hollow in Co. Kildare – a spot made famous by the legendary Dan Donnolly, the great bare-fisted fighter who in 1815 and at that spot, beat the English champion, George Cooper, in eleven rounds – breaking his jawbone. Donnolly was undoubtedly the greatest heavyweight in the world in his day. He was subsequently knighted by the Prince Regent – the last man to be so honoured during the Regency. In 1960, *The Ring* magazine put the final seal on Dan's greatness by recalling his deeds of almost a century and a half earlier and electing him to boxing's Hall of Fame.

By the time I was eleven years of age, there were seven children in the family and Dad had lost his job with the Merchant Warehousing Company. Silos – new technology – had been invented whereby the grain ships could be unloaded in hours rather than days. Men like my dad were no longer needed. On the dole, he received £1 a week. It meant economies.

Six mornings a week, I took a pillow-slip and queued with hundreds of other youngsters to buy the previous day's unsold bread at Kennedy's bakery on Ringsend Road. Five loaves (turnovers) could be had for a shilling. We had tea, bread and butter for breakfast on those mornings, while on Sunday mornings there was the luxury of an egg and rasher. We normally ate stew for dinner and, of course, Friday was fish day. I was frequently sent to buy fish to Maggie Caulfield's huckster shop in Thorncastle Street. Like the famed Biddy Mulligan of the song, Maggie had the fish laid out on the board – cod, ray, whiting and Dublin Bay herrings. A dozen herrings cost a shilling.

The greatest event in Dublin of those years was the staging of the Eucharistic Congress in the summer of 1932. The streets of the city were decorated with bunting and Papal flags seemed to fly from everywhere. Scores of thousands of people travelled to Dublin and the Phoenix Park was overflowing for the mass on the Saturday at which John McCormack sang "Panis Angelicus". It was a glorious spectacle and a most moving religious experience.

I took a terrible hammering in a fight with Tommy Halpin of the Corinthian Club in December 1933. He was an outstanding juvenile champion and won the junior flyweight title in 1938. Soon after the contest, I met a man named Eddie de Courcy, a former professional boxer. He was a pigeon fancier and came to buy some birds from my dad. Seeing my few boxing trophies, he asked me how I was progressing. I told him I was thinking of giving up the game as I had taken some stick in my last contest. He advised against doing so and offered to give me special training twice a week if I went to his house at Eblana Villas. I accepted his offer and he taught me weight-training, muscle control and body building. I regained my confidence.

Soon, I would be thirteen years of age. There was a long way to go.

2. A working man at fourteen

In 1933 my brother John and I joined St. Andrew's Boxing Club whose base was a large room in a Georgian house at 42 York Street, Dublin. Willie Carroll was in charge, aided by his son, also Willie. Carroll Snr. was a remarkable athlete who had his first fight early in the century at a fair in Brunswick Street (now Pearse Street). The promoter, Louis Smith, was so impressed by Willie's boxing ability that he advised him to take up the game seriously. Sgt. Major Mordaunt, a Wexford man and a keen boxing enthusiast, opened a boxing club. Willie Carroll joined that club and soon afterwards won the featherweight title at the first ever Irish amateur boxing championships which were held at Dublin's ancient concert rooms, later the Palace cinema.

St. Andrew's Club, which we had now joined, already had a splendid record, with a string of champions to its name, including Mattie Rogers, George Collins, Paddy Byrne and the inimitable Ernie Smith who won the first of his eight Irish senior titles in 1932. He was truly one of the greats of Irish amateur boxing. In later years, I remember Ernie, Brendan Behan and John "Spike" McCormack (of whom I will be writing later) being great friends – spending many hours together playing snooker in Jackie Mulvaney's Home of Billiards and then going on for a few pints in Davy's Bar on Eden Quay.

Jack Kennedy was another of St. Andrew's greats, as were

Tommy Byrne and Paddy Gernon. Paddy won five Irish
championships and had a marvellous international career.
Tommy Byrne suffered only two defeats in the four years from
December 1934 to December 1938. Both were international
bouts. One was against that splendid English fighter Ernie
Shackleton. Joe Rock, father of singing star Dickie Rock, was
another St. Andrew's boxer. He won the junior featherweight
title in 1934 and went on to wear the Irish singlet in international competition.

But in many ways, perhaps the most phenomenal of St.
Andrew's boxers was Ollie Byrne. He joined the club in 1939
and won the junior welterweight title in 1948. He won the
senior light-middleweight title in 1954 and the light-heavyweight title in 1957, 1958, 1959, 1961 and, incredibly, again in
1967 – 35 years after he had joined the club. Ollie was still
boxing in club shows in 1974. Although he worked at
Guinness' brewery, Ollie never drank; he was also a non-
smoker. Today he is as fit as ever and imparting his vast
knowledge to the boys of the Greenhills Club in Walkinstown.

And here's a name all will be familiar with – Eamonn
Andrews. He, too, was a St. Andrew's Club boy. As a lad, he
was very tall – nearly six feet when he joined the club. He won
an all-Ireland juvenile title and then went on, in 1945, to take
the junior middleweight title. By then he was already doing
boxing commentaries on Radio Eireann. Alas, St. Andrew's
Club is no more.

But back to life in Dublin in the mid-thirties. By now there
were nine children in our family – seven boys and two girls.
Times were bad. My father was still unemployed, as were so
many more. Eventually he was put on an employment
scheme, working three days a week for Dublin Corporation
and signing on the dole for the other three days. In those
days, most families were large and many were living with
their in-laws.

My grandfather Ingle figured large in those years of my
boyhood. He was quite a character. He was born in London in

1875 and, as a sailor, came to Dublin where he courted my grandmother and married her in Ringsend Catholic Church. He became more Irish than the Irish themselves. But even when he no longer was a young man he had quite an eye for the ladies. As a boy I met him one day coming from McCormack's pub in Bath Avenue, accompanied by a good-looking blonde lady. Putting a finger to his lips he said to me: "You have not seen me, James." I hadn't.

Every Saturday my grandfather was to be found drinking pints of Guinness in Peter Nort's in Ringsend. He had an amazing repertoire of Irish ballads and while he sang the pints kept coming. At closing time, he was invariably drunk and arrived home on unsteady legs to be greeted with Gran's profanity: "Buddy ode bastad" (she had no dentures). But no matter what he had done, his dinner had been kept warm for him in the oven and he ate it with relish. On summer Sunday mornings he took us swimming at Sandymount Strand. In those days of the early thirties the tide came in to a granite breakwater stretching from Irishtown Road to Pigeon House Road. The beautiful strand was soon afterwards made a rubbish dump by Dublin Corporation and we had to walk for miles to the Sherry Banks, another lovely beach about a mile from the old Pigeon House Fort, a former British barracks commanding the mouth of the Liffey.

I had my first fight with St. Andrew's Club at Liverpool Stadium. My opponent was Gus Foran who, years later, beat Jackie Patterson, the world flyweight champion. I won on points. The next outing was in Mullingar where I out-pointed Maxie McCullagh. The following morning, a newspaper described it as having been a wonderful exhibition of boxing by "two potential champions". That forecast was a good one.

At about that time too, we got some new neighbours. My great-uncle, Charles Bridger, who lived next door at 48 Penrose Street moved to Britain Quay. He was a stableman, employed by the Merchant Warehousing Company and he wanted to be nearer to his job.

An Italian family moved in at No. 48. Their name was Martina. The father was a terrazzo craftsman and, in a few short months, he turned that small house into a little palace. They had a luxurious bathroom and toilet, as well as various other amenities which were unheard of in those days in working-class Dublin. We still washed in a galvanised bath in front of the coal fire in the living room. The same tub was used by my mother to wash our clothes. She used a wooden scrubbing board and carbolic soap. Francisco Martina, the elder of the two boys next door, was born in Italy. The younger boy was Gerald. He was born in Dublin. We became great pals and soon the newcomers were part of the scene – with the Chesters, Kellys, Purdys, Fitzsimmons, Doyles, Canavans, O'Reillys, Austins, Mannings and Hylands. We played football, handball and cricket in the street. Looking back, we were a remarkable bunch of youngsters. Gerald Martina became a great Irish heavyweight wrestling champion and represented the country in the Olympic Games. Arthur Fitzsimmons was a Shelbourne football player who became famous when he transferred to Middlesborough. He also, of course, played for Ireland. My brother Bernie and I represented our country in boxing.

Playing those games in the street meant being constantly hounded by the Gardai. Our two tormentors were nicknamed Duck Ass Dan and Ninety E. They gave us no respite as they chased us through the back lanes of Dock Street, Doris Street and Penrose Street. When they caught us, we received a kick in the backside or a clip around the ears with their heavy woollen gloves. There was very little vandalism in Dublin in those times. If we accidentally broke a neighbour's window playing football, our parents paid for the damage and belted us afterwards. It was rough justice, but it was effective and we always tried to keep out of trouble.

My brother John and I joined the men's sodality at Ringsend Catholic Church and attended the monthly meetings. Once a year, there was a week-long retreat. A missionary came and preached fire and brimstone and the pains of hell for all eternity if we continued in our evil ways. Strong men quailed as they were denounced for their drunkenness, adultery and wife-beatings. The pubs in Ringsend – Peter Nort's, Fagan's and Fitzharris' – did little business that week. Peter Ferrarie's fish and chipper did a roaring trade and was packed every night.

I first met David Stewart in October 1934, when he came to give my dad some advice on pigeon breeding. He was a Chaplinesque figure with a bowler hat, baggy trousers, boots and a small, black moustache. But he was to have a lot to do with my life for years to come. A Scot, he was born in Edinburgh around 1880 and during World War I was lucky to survive when a mortar bomb exploded in front of the trench, killing all his mates. David was badly injured, but his superb fitness saw him through a long period of convalescence. He was a professional boxer who met all of the best men at his weight before the war – including Arthur Evernden, Johnny Summers, Young Josephs and Seely of Mile End. He also excelled as a weightlifter and draughts player. He won an Irish draughts championship. On marrying a girl from Dublin, he settled there, living with his in-laws for many years.

To our young, impressionable minds, it was magic when he told the stories of the great fighters like Jimmy Wilde and Young Griffo. Every Monday, Wednesday and Friday evening, we went to St. Andrew's Boxing Club for training and, on the way home, David would explain how I could improve my skill with a simple move. He would demonstrate on the pavement to the amusement of passers-by.

I was still at school, in my last year. The teacher, Mr. Comerford, was a kindly man with a great sense of humour. By now, Dad was back in full-time employment. He was working with Thomas Gray, the haulage firm in Dock Street. When I left school, the manager of the firm, Toby Breslin, employed me as a horse-minder. My job was to hold the reins of a still not fully-trained animal while the driver unloaded artificial manure at the yard of the company Paul & Vincents. I

27

was a skinny lad, five-foot nothing and weighing only six stone. The horse towered above me and weighed nearly a ton. One day, a car backfired, and the frightened animal reared. Up I went with it. Next thing we were bolting down the quay. I hung on grimly. I was terrified that, if I let go, the horse's hooves would trample me to pulp or the cartwheels would cut me in two. A brave man, seeing my plight, ran alongside the horse, grabbed its mane and eventually brought it to a halt. Having established that I was uninjured, he advised me to get another job, adding: "You might not be so lucky next time".

A new job quickly presented itself. Looking back, it too was an unusual form of employment. The Electricity Supply Board was extending its generating station at the Pigeon House Fort. Steel girders, twenty feet long, were being driven into the sand to strengthen the foundations. When being transported by a horse-drawn wagon, these girders extended five or six feet beyond the length of the wagon. The law required somebody to walk behind to ensure that there wouldn't be an accident. That became my job. I walked behind the wagon from the North Wall to the Pigeon House, a journey of approximately eight miles, twice a day.

About that time too, Dublin Corporation allocated my parents a small cottage in Philomena Terrace, Stella Gardens, as the little house in Penrose Street had long been overcrowded. But there was no bathroom nor hot water there either. Still, it was a big improvement on our former circumstances. David Stewart and my father built a small gymnasium at the end of the yard where John and I trained two evenings a week in addition to our regular visits to St. Andrew's Club. I was fighting regularly and having good wins. But my job walking behind the wagon finished when the last piles were delivered to the Pigeon House Fort.

Then Matt Canavan, a sawyer employed by Packing Cases Ltd. of South Lots Road, told me that the firm was taking on boy labourers. I applied and was interviewed by Mr. Scally, the managing director. He took me on. The wage was ten shillings and nine pence (54p) a week – working forty-seven hours from Monday to Saturday. I worked with Paddy Smith, a sawyer who cut blocks of timber into lengths. I then carried the lengths to the men who made the packing cases – Johnny Campion, "Jockey" Sheridan, Sean Barret, "Twigger" Meade, Eugene Fitzsimmons and Jack Ivory.

The factory itself was a huge complex, built of steel girders and with a glass roof and concrete floor. We sweated profusely when the sun shone through that roof and through the windows. In winter time, it was like a fridge. There was no teabreak. We worked from 8.00 in the morning until 1.00p.m., when we had an hour's dinner break. We then resumed work and continued until 5.30p.m. Smoking wasn't allowed and a breach of that rule meant instant dismissal. Men desperate for a smoke often risked their jobs, dashing to the lavatory for a quick puff. And it was a risk. The lavatories were without doors and Mr. Scally regularly strolled through the factory like a sergeant-major on parade. The men kept their heads down and worked hard.

We were unionised, but all our shop stewards did was collect the weekly union dues. We did, however, have one strike during my seven years there. It was when the labourers asked for a penny an hour increase. It was rejected immediately. The sawyers and casemakers continued working while the rest of us picketed the factory. Mr. Scally contemptuously drove the firm's lorry, loaded with the completed wooden boxes, through the picket lines. We did nothing to stop him delivering. Within a week, we were back at work.

Emmet McCabe and I worked at the same bench. One day, Emmet's apron string tangled with the feed wheel driving the timber through the circular saw which sped at thousands of revolutions a minute. I will always remember the look of horror on his face as he struggled desperately to free himself. Slowly, he was being drawn towards that spinning saw and to a horrific death. I was rooted to the ground, paralysed with terror at the prospect of seeing my friend sliced like a piece of timber. But there was somebody more experienced to hand. Paddy Smith jumped over a table, gripped the starting handle of the machine and knocked off the power. Poor Emmet collapsed on the floor.

3. Champion of Europe

In 1936 the Ingle family moved house again – to Margaret Place, Bath Avenue. It was a modern, semi-detached house with a bathroom. Once again David Stewart and my father built a gymnasium for us. It was well equipped with a heavy punchbag, floor-to-ceiling speed ball and a springball presented to me by Mr. Farrell, a pigeon-fancier friend of Dad's. This latter piece of equipment cost about £10, a huge sum in those days. It was a most generous gesture by a man who followed my boxing career until my final fight.

I will always remember a tournament held in the summer of 1937 at the Oblate Fathers' grounds in Inchicore. The proceeds went towards the building of the National Stadium. I was chosen to box English schoolboy champion Basil Magee from Liverpool. He was trained by the legendary Nel Tarlton, a former British professional champion who won outright two Lonsdale Belts.

We boxed four rounds and, after a great battle, I was awarded the verdict on points. I collected my prize, a beautiful bone-handled carving set. Feeling very pleased with myself, I returned to the tent which was used as a dressing room. I was looking forward to giving the carving set to my mother.

Then there was an announcement over the loudspeaker asking Magee and me to return to the ring. We did and the MC declared that one of the judges had made an error on his score card and that the decision was being reversed. Magee was the winner. So I had to hand back the carving set.

Afterwards David Stewart said to me: "Never mind, Jimmy. You boxed very well. Magee was a very good opponent. If you continue as you are doing, you will win the Irish flyweight championship in 1939 and also the European title."

I looked at him in amazement, but he went on to tell me that in two years' time the National Stadium would be completed and that the 1939 European championships would be staged there. If I was prepared to continue training six days a week, I would be the first Irishman to win a European title, he told me. As I was still only fifteen years of age, it seemed an extravagant forecast. But David was most insistent. He pledged to supervise all my training and guide me in living a spartan life. I promised to do my very best.

After winning the 1938 flyweight championship, Paddy Connolly retired. He was probably the greatest flyweight Ireland ever produced. He had boxed all over the world. In November 1934, he beat the British Empire and European champion, Pat Palmer, in Belfast. Two years later, Palmer fought Benny Lynch for the world professional title. Paddy's win over Lennie Cohen in the Golden Gloves tournament in Chicago in 1933 resulted in his being installed as "Chief Little Thunder". It was an honour which Paddy cherished and which immensely impressed the rest of us. The only other Irishman to have received such an honour was Eamon de Valera.

Paddy told me of his world travels and of the famous people he had met and the wonderful life which boxing had given him. "You are just starting your career; mine is finished. But I can look back with great pleasure and pride," he said. They were inspiring words.

I boxed my first junior fight in October 1936, beating Willie Gifford. Soon afterwards I was matched with Dave Coffey who, only a few weeks earlier, had beaten B. J. Fisher of England in an international bout. I won impressively on points at Portabello. Early the following year, I won the junior flyweight title and then entered for the senior championship. In the first bout, I was drawn against Johnny Healy, who first boxed for Ireland in 1934 and won the senior flyweight title in 1937. He and Paddy Connolly had some mighty battles. I weighed only seven stone, ten pounds on the morning of the weigh-in.

The National Stadium was now open and the championships were taking place there for the first time. It was a marvellous arena and still is. But, back in 1939 it was unique, the only one in the world to be owned by a national amateur boxing association. A lot of very able people of vision had put tremendous work into having the stadium built. Among its trustees was a senior government minister, Frank Aiken. I beat Johnny Healy in what was a great battle. Thereafter it wasn't too difficult and I emerged as senior champion.

A few days later I was picked for the flyweight berth in an international against Scotland which took place at the National Stadium on 16 March. My opponent was Johnny Shaughnessy, who was being spoken of as a future Benny Lynch. To add to my delight, I was named captain of the Irish team. You can imagine how proud I felt as I walked down the gangplank to the ring centre, carrying aloft the Irish tricolour. Then the National Anthem was played and the crowd sang. I beat Shaughnessy on points over six rounds.

The European championships were scheduled for Dublin a month later. It was the biggest international sporting occasion which Ireland had ever hosted. It was taking place at a time when fears of World War II were mounting.

In a recollection series for the *Irish Independent,* that fine sports correspondent Arthur MacWeeney, himself a qualified boxing judge, wrote:

The dark shadow of World War II, which was soon to open its floodgates of horror and misery, lay heavy over Europe and the championships took place in an atmosphere of suspicion and warped judgement which, for a sporting event, had no parallel in my memory.

Time after time during that uneasy week, contests were decided with a blatant disregard for what happened in the ring. Judges were swayed far more by what country a man came from than by any question of his skill.

The Juré d'Appel met almost nightly, reversing decisions in which the most outrageous travesties of justice had occurred, sacking officials, and trying to sooth the ruffled feelings of others who were threatening to withdraw their teams.

That's a very accurate description of how it was.

But, whatever animosities, boxers came to Dublin from all over Europe and they included Olympic, European and, of course, national champions. The opening night was one of great pageantry and excitement as the teams marched into the ring with banners held proudly high. The Irish army band played "The Soldier's Song" and again the crowds sang it with fervour.

The Irish weren't expected to do very well. Compared with the punching power of Germany, Britain, Italy, Poland, Sweden and the rest, we seemed a modest bunch. I made my debut against Belgian Jan Engelen and kept the fight at long range. I won decisively and was given a rapturous reception.

But we had lots of casualties. Miley Doyle, at bantamweight, lost to Bondi of Hungary. It was a very bad decision. Doyle seemed a clear winner. Paddy Gernon, boxing with a poisoned finger, lost narrowly to Kanepe of Estonia and our light-heavyweight champion, Joe Boyd from Northern Ireland, arrived late for the weigh-in and was eliminated without throwing a punch.

On the Wednesday evening, we did better, winning two of our three contests. Paddy Dowdall boxed superbly to beat the German Anton Traaf, while Charlie Evenden skilfully out-pointed Rossi of Finland. Our lone defeat that evening was in the heavyweight division where Jack McMullan from Banbridge, who had been picked instead of the reigning Irish champion, Corkman Paddy O'Sullivan, fought with great courage against the reigning European champion, Olle Tanberg of Sweden. Despite conceding two stone in weight and six inches in height, Jack fiercely attacked the giant but took a beating in the last two rounds. Before the verdict was announced, Jack walked over to Tanberg's corner and, taking the Swede's hand, raised it in victory. It was a splendid gesture by a man who didn't take a backward step in that fight.

The following night, I was in action again – against Giovanni Nardeccia of Italy, who was the favourite to take the flyweight title. The stadium was packed. Even when I was going in, there was a huge crowd inside. Many shouted encouragement and greetings to me. Paddy Connolly was in the dressing room and gave me a massage. Then I went down the gangway and into the ring. Nardeccia was already there, shadow-boxing in his corner. I could see the muscles rippling under his olive skin.

He attacked immediately, throwing punches from all angles. I slipped most of them over my shoulders and put in some good counters to the body. I heard him grunt. Using a good straight left in the second round, I continually jolted his head back. The blood began to flow from his nose and down his vest. As the round ended, I caught him with a left hook. It was a shade high on the cheek-bone, but it still bounced him into his own corner as the bell rang.

I felt fine coming out for the last round and my left beat a continuing tattoo on his battered nose. He put in a grandstand finish, but without troubling me. As I went back to my corner, I could see Willie Carroll's face beaming with pleasure. He threw his arms around my shoulders and said: "Great, Jimmy, you've won well."

The MC collected the judges' scoring cards and, after checking them, looked a bit puzzled. He checked them again and then announced the verdict – Nardeccia, on points. For some seconds there was an extraordinary silence. Then pandemonium broke loose. Howls of anger seemed to rock the building. The clamour continued and got louder and louder. By now, I was back in the dressing room. One of the Irish officials, Mick Hayes, rushed in and asked me to return to the ring and appeal to the fans to let the bouts continue.

I walked back down the gangplank, climbed into the ring held up my hands and succeeded in getting silence. "Gentlemen," I said, "please be quiet and let the bouts go on." But my appeal was in vain. The uproar resumed and I was quickly ushered back to the dressing room. It continued for nearly half an hour and all of the time there was the fear of a riot. Unknown to me, the Juré d'Appel was re-examining the judges' papers. Its members reached a unanimous decision that there had been an injustice and that I had won. This announcement was duly made and greeted with prolonged applause. The championships then proceeded.

The finals took place on Saturday, 22 April, and two of us were still in contention: Paddy Dowdall and myself. I was on first. My opponent was Nikki Obermauer of Germany. He tried to hustle me out of it, bundling me into the ropes. But, using my left hand, I was soon catching him and side-stepping. He was missing with his best punches. I decided to keep the bout at long range.

So it continued for three rounds. Only once was I forced to mix it. That was in the last half-minute of the fight when he trapped me in a neutral corner and nearly broke my ribs with powerful body blows. The fans were silent. But then I caught him and knocked him into a corner where I had him trapped. I drove home blow after blow to his weary body throughout the remaining seconds of the fight.

Again there was the long wait for the verdict. Then it came: "Winner and European flyweight champion – Ingle of Ireland." The largely partisan crowd stood on their seats cheering. Hats, caps, programmes and newspapers were tossed into the air. Obermauer came over to my corner and congratulated me. He was a good sport and the crowd acknowledged him as he left the ring. Frank Aiken, then Irish Minister for Defence, put the European belt around my waist. They played the National Anthem and that was that.

Paddy Dowdall was sitting in the dressing room. "Jimmy did it and I can do it too," he said quietly. Nobody gave him a chance against Poland's Anton Czortek, who had decisively won all his fights. But Dowdall confounded them all, displaying inspired ringcraft. The last round was a classic. Czortek, knowing that he was behind, attacked from the bell. Instead of retreating, Dowdall slugged it out with him punch for punch. It was really fierce. After what seemed an eternity, the bell rang ending the fight. Paddy Dowdall was champion of Europe, too.

This time the crowd celebrated so lustily that it appeared the roof might lift. It was a truly great night for Irish sport. Its significance can be seen in the fact that, in the forty-five years since then, Ireland has won only two more European amateur boxing titles.

So, there I was, still only seventeen years of age and the first Irishman ever to be champion of Europe.

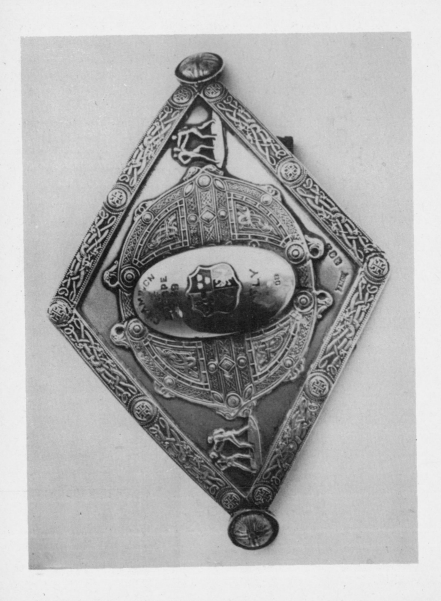

Front panel of the European Championship belt.

Charlie 'Hoppy' Ingle, Jimmy Ingle and David Stewart on 22 April 1939.

4. An offer from Gene Tunney

After the European amateur championships the eight new champions were required to go to the United States to compete in the Golden Gloves International. But I was unable to travel. I had obtained two weeks leave of absence from work for the European championships, but I could not get a further four weeks leave for the American trip. Ollie Lethenin took my place. The tournament took place in Chicago on 12 May and Europe won by five bouts to three. Lethenin won his contest, as did my fellow-Dubliner Paddy Dowdall. He beat Ray Lewis and became the unofficial amateur featherweight champion of the world. I was naturally disappointed that I didn't have the chance of doing likewise. But there were compensations.

The lads at work presented me with a gold wristwatch inscribed: "To Jimmy Ingle, European Flyweight Champion 1939 – from Packing Cases Ltd," It was a nice gesture from a great crowd of workmates.

Then Johnny McManus, the Scottish featherweight champion, came to box in Dublin. He was accompanied by his manager, the legendary Ted Broadribb, whose many distinctions in the ring included being the only Englishman ever to beat the Great Georges Carpentier of France. McManus was training at St Andrew's gymnasium and I was invited to spar with him. Much to the surprise of Ted Broadribb, I more than held my own. Johnny responded by putting on pressure and I retaliated. This angered him and he came at me throwing punches from all angles. I found him an open target and dumped him on the canvas with a quick right counter. Broadribb was amazed to see his protégé on the floor and afterwards asked me where I had learned to hit with such power. I told him of my success in the Irish and European amateur championships and he said I could make a lot of money in the professional ranks. He added that, if my parents were agreeable, he would be willing to manage my affairs.

I was all for it and my parents didn't object. So, it was arranged that after I returned from America, where I was to box with the Irish team in Chicago in July, I would turn professional. Ted Broadribb then put up all the expenses so that I might visit London for a fortnight and obtain some first-class experience of sparring with professionals.

I certainly did get experience. The first professional I sparred with was Henry Armstrong, who was training at Clacton for a defence of his world welterweight title against Ernie Roderick. It was, of course, an immense honour. Armstrong was, simultaneously, featherweight, lightweight and welterweight champion of the world — a record which will never be broken because the boxing authorities subsequently introduced a rule whereby a man could hold but one world title at the same time.

Armstrong was a phenomenon — undoubtedly one of the greatest fighters of all time. In October 1937, he knocked out Peter Sarron in six rounds to capture the world featherweight title. Then, the following May, he beat Barney Ross on points over fifteen rounds to take the welterweight title. Ross was so badly punished by Armstrong that he never boxed again. Henry then reverted to nine stone, nine pounds and beat Lou Ambers on points in August 1938 to add the lightweight crown. So it was that, from October 1937 to December 1938, when he relinquished the featherweight crown, Armstrong was holder of three championships at the same time. And, of course, there were only eight divisions in those days.

So, here I was, only seventeen years of age and sparring with Henry Armstrong. We boxed three rounds. He never tried to land a damaging punch. Afterwards, he asked me to do another couple of rounds with his sparring partner, Chalkey Wright. Chalkey was one of the greatest characters I have ever met. He kidded me, tied me in knots, and, with a big grin, stuck out his chin invitingly. In desperation, I threw a short right which landed dead on target. His eyes rolled and his hands dropped momentarily before he grabbed me and wrapped his arms around my shoulders. Then shaking his head, he said: "Oh boy, that shu did hoit." We became very good friends.

I went to Haringey Arena on 25 May and saw Armstrong defend his title against Ernie Roderick. It was a marvellous night and the first world title fight that I had witnessed. Round after round, Armstrong pounded Roderick's body. It was as if he were driving rivets. Soon, Ernie's body was covered with red blotches. But he still stayed the course. At the final bell, he slumped exhausted on the stool. The verdict was a formality. Armstrong's purse that night was £8,500 – a huge sum in boxing in those days. How times have changed!

Chalkey Wright beat George Daly in the main supporting bout. Daly too stayed the distance – a most gallant performance against a man who, two years later, in September 1941, knocked out Joey Archibald to win the world feather-weight title.

I greatly enjoyed my visit to London and, in saying goodbye to Ted Broadribb, I pledged that I would be back in September to turn professional.

Ahead lay a magical trip to the United States. This time I was able to get leave from work. There were ten boxers on the Irish team – myself at flyweight; Miley Doyle (bantam); Peter Glennon and Jack Gafney (feather); Paddy Gernon (light); Charlie Evenden and John "Spike" McCormack (welter); Fred Price (middle); Steve Sullivan (light-heavy); and Paddy

O'Sullivan (heavy). Dick Hearns, who had retired after a wonderful career, was nominated our trainer.

The team assembled at the then Kingsbridge station, Dublin on Monday, 5 July, and with our families and hundreds of well-wishers waving us goodbye, we left for Cobh, Co. Cork, to embark for America on the liner *Samare*. It was a wonderful voyage – although a few of the lads had spells of seasickness. Peter Glennon was worst affected.

Dick Hearns was a very strict trainer. He had us all up at 7 o'clock each morning and running around the deck for an hour. Later in the day we participated with other passengers in deck tennis and in the evening there were two hours in the gymnasium. Each night we went to bed exhausted.

Although I was training hard, my weight was increasing dramatically – touching on the bantamweight limit of eight stone, six pounds. For a time, it looked as if I would have to concede the bout to my American opponent. Then Miley Doyle intervened. He offered to make the flyweight limit of eight stone, saying to me: "You are young and growing quickly. It would damage your health to take off nearly half a stone." It was a most caring and generous gesture on the part of a great sportsman.

Soon the Statue of Liberty was in sight, and then New York itself. In these days of colour television and Concorde New York is visually commonplace. But back in 1939 it was an unbelievable spectacle: the Empire State Building; our trip down Broadway; visiting Jack Dempsey's restaurant; and the rest. And what a welcome! For two days we were fêted by Irish organisations in New York and Boston. Then, singing songs and with more than a few tears, they saw us off to our destination, Chicago.

We arrived there to another tumultuous reception. Thousands of people lined the route from the railway station to our hotel and they were waving the Irish and American flags. Ticker tape cascaded like snowflakes from the buildings on to the open coach in which we were travelling. What needs to be remembered is that it was a great and rare event for the Irish in the United States in those days to have the opportunity of welcoming a sports team from Ireland.

No fewer than 35,000 people came to Soldiers Field, Chicago, that night to see Ireland box the champions of the Catholic Youth Organisation (representing Catholic clubs, universities and schools throughout the US). To add to the occasion, the referees were former world heavyweight champion Gene Tunney and the reigning champion, Joe Louis.

It ended in a draw – five bouts all. As he had promised to do, Miley Doyle made the flyweight limit and not alone that but won his bout. I won at bantam. The other Irish winners were Glennon, McCormack and O'Sullivan. I was deemed the best boxer on the Irish team and presented with a gold-plated cup.

After my contest with Frank Basoune, Gene Tunney came into the dressing room and told me I had boxed well. He told me that he was particularly impressed with my straight left, the punch he himself had perfected. We talked a little more and then he said: "If you would like to stay in America and turn professional, I will look after your welfare."

Tunney, who had earned a massive fortune in his two heavyweight title victories over Jack Dempsey was, by 1939, a successful buisnessman. He later went on to become president of a huge corporation and his son, John, became a US senator. He was a sophisticated and cultured man of Co. Mayo stock who, even in his boxing days, communicated regularly with Bernard Shaw. To have had Tunney as one's mentor in America would have counted for a lot. But I had already given my word to Ted Broadribb. I explained this to Gene Tunney and thanked him sincerely. He wished me luck.

Two days later, 21 July 1939, was my birthday. I was eighteen years old. It was a marvellous day. The Irish party was taken on a tour of Chicago which included flying in an aeroplane. Needless to say, it was my first such experience. I will always remember how exhilarating it was gazing down in wonder at the city below and at beautiful Lake Michigan with its waves lapping the shore.

When we returned to the hotel, I received what remains the greatest surprise of my life. On the dining-room table was a huge birthday cake. The hotel orchestra was in position and the waiters and waitresses all gathered round and began singing "Happy Birthday". The lads on the team, some of whom must have known of the preparations, began shaking my hand and offering congratulations. I had never before had a birthday party and I just couldn't stop the tears flowing.

We arrived home in Dublin to a tremendous welcome. Although it was 2 o'clock in the morning, hundreds of people welcomed us at Kingsbridge. There was a taxi ready to take me to my own home in Ringsend. When I arrived there, there were thousands of people from all over the district cramming into the surrounding streets. I was carried shoulder-high by neighbours down Bath Avenue and I saw a banner proclaiming "Welcome Home Jimmy" across Margaret Place. The beer flowed freely until dawn and there was singing and dancing. Even now almost forty-five years later, when I return home on holiday, people still remind me of that night.

Those were drab years. A lot of people found joy in having something to celebrate and take pride in. A local lad had gone to America and brought home the cup.

There was also a telegram from Ted Broadribb offering congratulations and saying he would be over in Dublin in September to finalise our agreement.

Soon afterwards, Frank Cooper and Jimmy Healy came to the house and asked me if I would join the Gardai. I was flabbergasted. For one thing, I stood not much above five feet. All the Gardai whom I knew were six-footers. But they told me that Tommy Maloney, the legendary Garda Boxing trainer, would soon be retiring and the authorities thought I would make an ideal replacement. As I mentioned earlier the Gardai were then committed to amateur boxing and Tommy Maloney was instrumental in producing a string of champions. They won no fewer than forty-two Irish championships from

1924 to 1938.

This was a marvellous offer. It meant a secure pensionable job for life. Not alone that, but I would be doing something for which I clearly had a talent. It would have been a big promotion from working as a boy labourer at less than £1 a week in a sawmill. But I had given my word to Ted Broadribb. I told them this regretfully. They shook hands with me and wished me luck in my future career.

So, now I had turned down not alone Gene Tunney but also a state job. But, not to worry! Ted Broadribb was coming to Dublin in a few weeks' time. I would return to London with him and begin the professional boxing career for which I was destined. In every sense, I was ready for it.

But Ted Broadribb didn't come over in September. What came, before he was due to arrive, was World War II.

5. Lost dreams and the end of an era

The outbreak of World War II early in September 1939 shattered my dreams. There would be no London now, certainly not as had been planned. And, of course, I had turned down Gene Tunney's offer. The United States wasn't at war but it was awfully far away. I had also turned down the opportunity to join the Gardai to become trainer of its great boxing club. Even the Olympic Games, due the following year, were now gone by the board. I was isolated. Looking back, it is possible to put things in perspective. They were but the shattered dreams of a teenager at a time when millions of other young men across Europe were destined for a far worse fate.

In Dublin life went on, and so did amateur boxing. I was back at the National Stadium in October for a great battle with my friend Myles Doyle. I won on points and the *Irish Press* correspondent said it was "Ingle's toughest fight yet". A crowd of almost 4,000 wildly cheered us that night.

The following Monday, Mr. Scally called me into his office at Packing Cases Ltd. and offered me an apprenticeship as a sawyer. It meant an increase of a pound a week in my wages.

There were more fights at the National Stadium — club tournaments. In January 1940, there was the inevitable return bout with Miley Doyle. Again the stadium was packed and we treated the fans to another great fight. For six rounds we battled for supremacy, neither of us prepared to retreat. The

47

fans roared themselves hoarse. I was again victorious. Miley and I walked back to the dressing room, arms around each other's shoulders.

In February, a month before the senior championships, I was cross-cutting hardwood when the saw jammed. Instead of knocking off the power, I foolishly tried to pull the timber away. The saw freed and, in a split second, the thumb and forefinger of my left hand were nearly severed. Mickey Behan, my assistant, ran to the office for the medical kit and told Mr. Scally that there had been a serious accident and to phone for an ambulance. As luck would have it, Mickey had trained in first aid and he skilfully bandaged the lacerated fingers, after putting a tourniquet on my arm. The surgeon successfully stitched the finger and thumb and assured me that I would be fit to box again in a couple of months.

My club-mate Sean Tallon won the 1940 flyweight title and I was delighted when Miley Doyle won the bantamweight division – his first title. For years Frankie Kerr had dominated that division. Paddy Dowdall, who had also won the European title the previous April, took, as was to be expected, the featherweight championship. It was his first Irish senior title also. Ernie Smith made a great comeback to take the light-weight title for the seventh time. Paddy Gernon moved up to welter and took over from Charlie Evenden. In doing so, he equalled Paddy Hughes' record of winning Irish titles at three different weights. Spike McCormack just failed to make the welterweight limit of ten stone, seven pounds, and elected to try for middleweight honours. He was successful. Frank Parsons from Galway took the light-heavy title and L. O'Donnell from Clonmel won the heavyweight division.

Meanwhile, the war was going badly for Britain and her allies. Belgium, France and Holland had been overrun. In Dublin we were issued with gas masks and rationing was introduced. There were coupons for butter, tea and clothing. But the Irish sense of humour prevailed and light was made of these difficulties. The Twenty-six Counties were, of course, neutral. But the Germans accidentally bombed Dublin's North Strand, devastating houses and killing many people.

Eventually I made a return to boxing, with Jack Gaffney making me work very hard for a decision. The next one was against Peter Glennon. It was a natural pairing, pending for some time. In the third round Peter caught me spot on the button with a beautiful right hand. I landed on my backside. The count reached nine. But I made it. I was dazed and Peter hit me with every punch in the book. I was glad to hear the bell. It was the first time in any contest that I had found myself on the floor. As my trainer and mentor, David Stewart, sponged me with cold water, he told me to act dazed. "When the round starts, Peter will try to finish the fight quickly and will leave himself open," he said.

That's how it ended. Peter charged from his corner like a tornado. He was open for a right counter, which stopped him in his tracks. The left hook which followed finished the fight. It was the first time in his entire career that Peter had been stopped.

My reward for that fight was a fifty-shilling voucher. With it I bought a suit from Premier Tailors in Henry Street. Clothing coupons were no problem, as Frankie Kerr was the manager of the shop. Frankie was one of the most courteous men ever to grace a boxing ring and the best bantamweight ever produced in Ireland. When I say that, I am including Willie Lenehan, Dave Connell and Freddie Gilroy and even Mick Dowling, who won eight Irish bantamweight titles. In an international career which stretched from 1932 to 1938, Frankie lost on only three occasions. He won six Irish senior titles — as a flyweight in 1932 and, thereafter, as a bantamweight. A wonderful exponent of the noble art, he died some years ago but is remembered with affection by the Irish boxing fraternity.

There were some really great characters in the Dublin of those years. One of them was "Cyclone" Billy Warren, an Australian black, who, in his day, boxed some of the greatest heavyweights the world has ever known, including Jack

Johnson. He also drew, over 25 rounds, with the great Peter Jackson in Melbourne in 1899. Having sampled America, Cyclone came to Europe and fought all over the place before deciding to settle in Dublin. He knocked out Jim Roche of Wexford to win the Irish heavyweight title. Roche, who, of course, had a short-lived world title fight with Tommy Burns, later regained that Irish title. Cyclone was still boxing at the age of fifty. When I became aware of him, he was very much a veteran, but still a most imposing figure as he walked from his home in Parnell Square down O'Connell Street, majestically surveying us tiny mortals from his lofty perch. He must have been nearly six feet, six inches. I never had the courage to ask him about his exploits as we held him in awe.

Alfie Byrne was Lord Mayor of Dublin during many of those years. He was a small, elegant man with a waxed moustache and twinkling eyes. He wore a bowler hat and pinstriped trousers. He rode around the city on a bicycle – the pinstriped trousers being held by bicycle clips. He was much loved and had a great concern for the city's poor.

Then there was Bang Bang, who was always jumping on the trams, and with a large door key in his right hand, shouting at the conductors: "Bang, Bang, you're dead". He then, unfailingly, laughed his head off as he ran from the scene. Everybody smiled at his antics, remembering that they too once played Cowboys and Indians. Bang Bang had never grown up.

Hector Gray came to Dublin from Scotland and soon became another of the city's characters. Every Sunday morning at the Halfpenny Bridge, he sold everything from needles to anchors. He would turn up with suitcases filled to overflowing and begin his spiel. Within an hour, he had unfailingly sold out. He went on to build a fine business and, although now very much a veteran, he is still trading from his shop.

But back to boxing. Jimmy Smith from Clonmel won the junior featherweight championship in 1939, but lost to Jack Gaffney in the senior division. He beat Jack in a return on a club show and then, sensationally, beat Paddy Dowdall and

Peter Glennon, breaking Peter's jaw in the process. Would Jimmy Ingle be his next victim?

There wasn't an empty seat in the National Stadium for our fight. Ticket touts had done excellent business, selling at double the price. For me, it was a disastrous fight. I could do nothing right. I was sluggish and my feet were like lead. I had over-trained. Jimmy got the decision.

By now I was, of course, a featherweight. Despite training conscientiously, I was putting on weight which, despite my lack of inches, eventually brought me up to middleweight.

My next battle was against Paddy Dowdall and it was an exceptional pairing. We were both reigning European champions. The press called it the "fight of the century". That's a cliché now. It wasn't then. It was a six-rounder and the Stadium was packed. Reporting for the *Irish Independent*, Arthur McWeeney wrote: "Not since they won the European titles have they performed so gloriously." The heading on the article was "Ingle A Wonder Boxer".

After that, a return bout with Jimmy Smith was inevitable. It's more than forty years since our second fight, but it remains as fresh in my memory as if it were yesterday. Half-way through the fourth round, I dropped my left hand and a right cross smashed on my jaw — the very same punch with which Jimmy had broken Peter Glennon's jaw. It dumped me into my own corner. The referee turned to the timekeeper to take up the count and I instinctively got to my feet. Then I felt a hand grip my ankle. Immediately, I dropped on one knee just before the referee could see what had taken place. But virtually everybody else in the stadium had seen David Stewart's action. I stayed down until the count reached nine. Then the bell went.

The Stadium was in uproar. Smith's father, who was also his second, demanded my disqualification. But the referee dismissed his appeal and told us to "box on". But for David's quick action in grabbing my ankle, I would have been back in the fight after a count of "one" and in no position to defend myself. I would have been knocked out. I recovered during the interval and, boxing on the retreat for the remaining two rounds, lasted the distance. But Jimmy was a good winner.

When the 1941 championships came I was four pounds over the featherweight limit and entered at lightweight. In the final I came up against Jack Draper, who was in the army and soon to be a lieutenant. He was very tall and, for a time, his long reach kept me at bay. But I stopped him in the second round.

Over the years, my nose had been giving me a lot of trouble. At one stage, I had minor surgery at Sir Patrick Dun's Hospital to relieve a minor blockage. But despite this it was becoming increasingly difficult to breathe properly. During contests, I frequently discarded my gumshield to breathe through my mouth. This often resulted in opponents driving my teeth through my lips – a very painful experience.

Having won the 1941 lightweight title, I decided to have a check-up and it was established that I needed major surgery. I went into hospital immediately. It was a disaster – but not in the way you would expect.

I was wheeled in the usual way into the operating theatre and had a mask put over my face. I was told to breathe deeply. As I was breathing, not yet fully anaesthetised, I became convinced that I was being strangled. I reacted violently, jerking my head quickly and removing the mask. The anaesthetist grabbed my hair and I belted him on the chin. He fell on the floor, out like a light. The attendant at the foot of the operating table grabbed my legs. I kicked him so hard he went flying through the swing doors. By then, I was off the table. By then, too, reinforcements had arrived. The scene which followed was indescribable. I went berserk and was throwing punches at everything that moved. In such a confined space, it was impossible to miss and soon half a dozen white-coated attendants were either stretched or staggering. But the exertion of it all – bearing in mind that I was already half anaesthetised – made me drowsy and, eventually, I was overcome and the operation commenced.

I was very sore afterwards. Dr. Powell, the assistant surgeon, told me it was the most difficult operation of its kind he had participated in as my cheek bones had become rock hard over the years from taking punches. He told me I was lucky to come through alive. Naturally, I apologised profusely for having gone berserk. All graciously forgave me, telling me that ether could have an unusual effect on some people; I wasn't responsible for my actions.

At the end of that year I left St. Andrew's Amateur Boxing Club and joined the Mount Street Club. There I was introduced to Dr. Peel, a governor of the club, who happened to be an ear, nose and throat specialist at the Adelaide Hospital. He told me more about the type of operation I had undergone. It was a double antrum operation, which involved slitting the flesh between the upper lip and nostrils, lifting the face to expose the bone structure and then cutting away the diseased parts. All is then stitched back. He told me that, as a young medic, he had been doing practice surgery for a double antrum operation on a corpse when the scalpel cut a fraction deeper than was necessary, resulting in the brains coming through the incision. A grim business!

But it was a beautiful summer and, in July, I boxed a return with Paddy Dowdall at the International Hotel in Bray. It was an open-air show in the spacious garden. It was a punishing and exhausting battle with the sun blazing down on top of us. When I came out for the fifth and final round, Paddy remained sitting disconsolately on his stool. He had no more to give. I went over and commiserated with him. It was the first time in his long and most distinguished career that he had not gone the full course. We were to fight again on three further occasions. I won two of them. In all, we fought five times and every fight was a sporting contest. Paddy Dowdall was one of Ireland's greatest-ever champions. He died a few years ago, having had a heart attack after playing a game of football in Dublin's Phoenix Park. In a fitting tribute, thousands of

Dubliners followed his cortège.

I boxed Jimmy a third time. Again, it was a battle. This time, I won. I was now nearing ten stone and boxing as a welterweight. Then came something which changed the entire course of events. George Flemming, president of the Irish Boxing Board of Control, asked David Stewart and me to call at his office in the Capitol Cinema (the old La Scala, where, back in 1923, Mike McTigue, from Co. Clare, beat Battling Siki for the world light-heavyweight title). It was a Saturday evening. We arrived at the arranged time and, over a cup of tea, George Flemming invited me to turn professional. He offered me £100 plus a guaranteed four contests at Dublin's Rotunda Cinema at £25 a fight. It doesn't sound an awful lot of money now, but back in 1942 it was. We agreed that I would make my professional debut in October.

I was twenty-one years of age. Some, with hindsight, would say that my professional prospects had long thinned out, that my time was back in 1939, as a bantamweight at the age of eighteen. I was now a stocky welterweight, lacking height and reach.

I still competed in that year's amateur championships — being beaten on points by Gerry Kilcullen in the welterweight final. By now, many former amateur champions had joined the professional ranks. Partly as a result of the war, the professional game had gained considerable momentum in Ireland with fights taking place regularly at venues up and down the country. I bade farewell to amateur boxing on 2 October 1942, against Spike McCormack at the National Stadium. Ironically, I was paid a tenner for that "amateur" fight. The Corinthians Club was putting on the show and an official from the club came to our house in Margaret Place and offered me £10 to box Spike on the bill. The fight was stopped in the third round when Spike collapsed on the ring floor. I was amazed, as I hadn't put him there. From the agonised look on his face, I knew something was radically wrong. I helped him to his corner. He was rushed to hospital where an emergency operation was performed on his hip. It had been shattered, I learned, during a raid on Dieppe. Spike had earlier joined the British army and was soon a commando. After being wounded, he was sent home to Dublin to recuperate. Later, I learned that the only reason he was on the Corinthian's bill was that he had been offered £30 to fight me.

That night I walked out of the National Stadium for the last time as an amateur boxer. In eleven years I had had 107 fights and had never been stopped. Virtually all of my most memorable fights took place at the Stadium. For me, it was the end of an era, of what life until then had been almost entirely about.

Jimmy Ingle in 1942 at the Capital Cinema, where he signed professional forms.

6. A bad night with Armour

For many years in Southern Ireland amateur boxing completely dominated, with the professional sport a very poor relation. Week after week the National Stadium was packed, as boxers from all Ireland engaged in combat and the fans came in their thousands to cheer their favourites. But World War II halted all international competition, including the European championships and the Olympics. Denied such opportunities, various boxers, who otherwise might not have done so, turned professional.

On Friday 9 October 1942, I made my professional debut at Dublin's Rotunda Cinema. It was packed, with hundreds outside unable to gain admission. Others on the bill included Pat Mulcahy, Jack Casey, Eddie Downey, Tommy Upton, Siki O'Neill, Pat Flynn and Jim Doran. My opponent was Chuck Flannigan from Northern Ireland. I stopped him in the second round.

Afterwards, Belfast promoter Bob Gardiner came into the dressing room and offered me six fights in Belfast at £15 a fight. I would have to pay my own expenses. I accepted. It was agreed that my first fight in Belfast would be on 17 October against Jim Hamilton from Carrickfergus, who was the number-one contender for the Ulster welterweight title.

At nine o'clock on that Saturday morning, David Stewart and I took the train from Dublin's Amiens Street station for

Belfast. David, who had done so much to guide my amateur career, was now my professional manager. Bob Gardiner met us as we came off the train in Belfast and he took us to Taylor's lodging house on Donegal Quay. The proprietor was a small, tubby man who smilingly shook hands and warmly welcomed us to his establishment – bed and breakfast, plus evening meal, for ten bob (50p). Later that evening David and I had our first experience of the wartime blackout. It was quite eerie. Total darkness enveloped everything: it was as if we were blind men being led to our destination, which was the Rialto on the Shankill Road.

There were long queues outside the building and I noticed that they included quite a number of American soldiers. By now, of course, the US had entered the war. On being introduced from the ring, I got a great cheer from the crowd and it proved to be a very good fight. It went the full eight rounds and I got the referee's nod. We were both cheered from the ring.

I had my third professional fight soon afterwards at Dublin's Rotunda, in which I knocked out Pat Kelly from Belfast in the second round. The fight of the night, however, was between Dubliners George Kelly and Tommy Cullen. It was a six-rounder and they savaged each other like terriers. Both collapsed on their corner stools at the end of a great fight and fully deserved the standing ovation when the referee declared it a draw. George Kelly subsequently settled in Corby, Northamptonshire. He is now the father of a grown family. But he is still remembered in Ireland as a great champion. He won the Irish amateur flyweight title in 1927, boxing for the Unity Club in Marlborough Street, once the headquarters of Jim Larkin. The following year George won the featherweight title. He also had, during that period, a number of fine international wins for Ireland. When he turned professional he won the lightweight title and his great battles with Patsy Quinn, Billy Gilmour and Johnny Ward are frequently recalled by those who witnessed them.

I had another win in Belfast – stopping Jim Doran – before, on 27 November, being paired with Patsy Quinn from Belfast at the Rotunda. Patsy was one of Ireland's greatest professional fighters throughout that era. He made his professional debut in 1933 and now had fifty paid fights under his belt. He gave me an awful hammering in the first round and was still working me over in the second until I caught him with a good right hand which halted him momentarily. Towards the end of the fight, I was hitting him with everything bar the corner stool, but he kept coming forward. We slogged it toe-to-toe in the final round. Such was the crescendo of cheering from the fans that we didn't hear the final bell and stayed belting each other until hauled apart by the referee. I got the verdict, but a draw would have been a better result. We walked from the ring, arms around each other's shoulders, with the fans still clapping and cheering.

On 5 December I was back in Belfast to box Andy McLoughlan from Derry. At the weigh-in he scaled eleven stone, six pounds; I was a stone lighter. It was a lot of weight to concede. Promoter Bob Gardiner gave me an extra £5 to go ahead and I did. It proved to be an easy fight: at the close of the fourth round McLoughlan retired.

I now had six professional victories, scored in the space of two months. Promoter Gardiner then floated the idea that I fight Northern Ireland welterweight champion Tommy Armour. I was agreeable, but David Stewart said it was too soon to meet a man regarded by many as the most destructive puncher in these islands. Armour had turned professional in January 1936 and at this stage had eighty-eight paid fights to his credit. He had won forty-three inside the distance, as well as twenty-five on points. Among his victims were former British welterweight champion Jake Kilrain and a whole string of men from the South, including Pat Mulcahy, Sean Clancy, Freddie Price, Jack Lenihan and Paddy Roche. After some discussion, we reached a compromise. I would fight Armour in Belfast on 20 March 1943, over ten rounds and my purse would be £25. Meanwhile, I would get as much additional professional experience as possible.

In the lead-up to Christmas, I had two more fights with Patsy Quinn – on 11 December and 19 December. Both were at the Rialto, Belfast, and over eight rounds. Both fights went the distance and I got the verdict.

But it was a sad Christmas for the Ingle family. Earlier in the year my seventeen-year-old brother Joe had a heart attack and was taken to Sir Patrick Dun's Hospital. Joe had contracted rheumatic fever as a child and it affected his heart so seriously that he was unable to attend school regularly or partake in our boyhood games. This made him very depressed. I remember one day when he said to me: "James, I would be better off if I were dead. My life is one continuous round of hospitals. I will never get well." Just before Christmas, Joe lapsed into a coma and we were told that he had only a short time to live. Every day we visited him. On 1 February my brother John was at his bedside all through the night; in the early hours of the morning, Joe passed away. It nearly broke my mother's heart, as a year previously she had lost a daughter who died three days after being born.

I was contracted to box Jim Josephs in Belfast the day after the funeral. I went ahead. Bob Gardiner had renamed the Rialto the Ulster Stadium and had put together a great supporting bill which included Rinty Monaghan fighting Harry Rodgers. Before my bout commenced, the MC announced that my brother Joe had died during the week. The large crowd stood in respect for a minute. I won the fight in the sixth round, with Josephs' corner throwing in the towel. I was back in Belfast later that month and had another inside-the-distance win, again in the sixth round.

I was still working in the sawmill eight and a half hours a day and it was hard work. The war had stopped the importation of timber and the country had to rely on native stock. It was delivered to the factory in its raw state of bark and sap. This meant it was very heavy. At the end of each day, I was tired from lifting and sawing those large, wet logs. I trained for two hours each night and then, after a shower and a cup of tea, went to bed. As soon as my head touched the pillow, I was in a deep sleep. My brother John was training equally hard for the senior amateur championships in March. He was near the lightweight limit and had developed a murderous left hook. We had some lively sparring sessions.

On the night of 20 March in Belfast I met Tommy Armour. He was the first southpaw I had ever boxed. As he came at me in response to the first bell, I threw a standard left lead. A left hook exploded on my jaw and bounced me into the ropes. He was on me like a tiger: short hooks to my body doubled me in agony. Then I noticed that something quite extraordinary was happening. The fans were on their feet howling like wolves. "Kill the bastard!" was the mildest of the exhortations. Most of the others had to do with maltreating the Pope and Catholics generally. I had never in my life heard anything like it. This was a venue in which I had boxed regularly since turning professional the previous October. Yet now, here was the Shankill mob howling like wolves for my blood. It was unbelievable and most disconcerting.

Armour gave me a frightful hiding. That left hand tore the flesh off my ribs and battered my face and ears into a swollen mass. Still the mob howled for more blood. The tenth and last round was a nightmare. I came out, seeing through a haze of blood which was flowing from a deep cut over my left eye. I staggered into another barrage of punches. To this day, I can't explain how I remained upright. But, as soon as the final bell sounded, I collapsed on the corner stool. The decision was a formality. Tommy Armour had won every round. But I had given a most courageous performance and, much to my surprise, the hostile crowd now applauded me back to the dressing room. I knew then how it must have felt for the Christian who somehow survived the Colosseum.

Promoter Bob Gardiner came into the dressing room afterwards and apologised to us. In addition to David Stewart, my dad was with me. Gardiner said he knew the louts who had engaged in the horrible sectarian baiting and that he would ban them from his shows in future.

Back in Dublin the next day, I got a taxi to Sir Patrick Dun's Hospital. There, the house surgeon inserted a needle into my ears and extracted the bruised blood. He worked on me for about half an hour and then said: "You will be all right now. You won't have cauliflower ears." He added that I wasn't to box again for a month.

In the finals of the amateur senior championships that same month, Paddy Dowdall won his second lightweight title, beating my brother John on points. It was a great battle. Gerry Coleman won the light-heavyweight title in those championships of 1943. It was the first of his record-breaking nine senior championships. He also, of course, after the war, won the European heavyweight title. Another fine winner in the 1943 championships was Mick Coffey, the Arbour Hill stalwart. He took the middleweight title. Mick won the first senior title, at welterweight, as far back as 1935. He was one of the most unassuming characters I have ever met, but a devastating puncher who scored magnificent victories against a string of American opponents during an extended visit to that country in 1938.

I was back in the Shankill three weeks after being hammered by Tommy Armour. This time my opponent was Sean Clancy, a fellow-Dubliner who had an outstanding amateur career which included splendid international victories at destinations as far distant as Boston, Hamburg and Warsaw. I won a very close decision. The Éire Boxing Board of Control, as it then was, nominated Sean and me to box for its vacant welterweight title, which Paddy Roche had relinquished to move up a weight. The date was set for 25 May and the venue was Dublin's Theatre Royal. But as it happened, Bob Gardiner had us booked for a return bout at his Ulster Stadium in the Shankill and this we duly went through with on 1 May. Again I got the verdict.

The big one was to be in Dublin and I had high hopes of becoming a professional champion. But it was not to be. Another accident at the sawmill intervened. Working on the spindle, rebating timber, the cutters struck a large knot. The wood jumped and my right hand was struck by the cutters, nearly severing the thumb and first three fingers of my right hand. A similar accident had cost me the amateur feather-weight title in 1940. Now I was denied my chance of the professional welterweight title. The surgeon did a masterly job of stitching the lacerated fingers. Later, I was told that I was very lucky. Had it been a little worse, it would have meant amputation.

The summer of 1943 was wonderful. Dad had an allotment in Herbert Park and John, who was a keen gardener, showed me how to plant potatoes and cabbages and lay seedbeds for beetroot, carrots, turnips and onions. Sonny Malloy, another allotment enthusiast, got us involved in turf-cutting in the Dublin Mountains. So, although out of action and prevented from training, I was in good shape looking after the allotment and cycling up the mountains to the bog.

Those not old enough to remember the war may be surprised to know that professional boxing shows continued in Britain during those frightful years. Nearly all the shows were in open-air arenas and always staged for charity, the promoter only retaining his costs. By 1943 many Irish boxers were performing regularly in England, among them Martin Thornton, Dom Lydon, Pat O'Connor and the late Paddy Roche. Paddy was a great one. Between 1937 and 1949, he had seventy professional fights against some of the best boxers in Britain, including Ernie Roderick, Dick Turpin, Don Cockell, Bert Gilroy, Vince Hawkins, Kid Berg, Dave McCleave, Arthur Danaher and Albert Finch. Paddy died in January 1978 in picturesque Wells, Somerset, at the age of sixty-five.

7. Revenge and a new job

My brother John made his professional debut in Belfast on 5 June 1943 with an impressive knockout victory. It resulted in promoter Bob Gardiner's including him on his next bill which was at the Cliftonville Football Ground, Belfast, on 13 July. Topping the bill was the pairing of Eric Boon and Tommy Armour. Boon was magic. In London, on 15 December 1938, he knocked out Dave Crowley in the 13th round to win the British lightweight title. The young blacksmith from Chatteris was only eighteen years of age – the youngest man ever to win a British title. The following February he successfully defended the title against Arthur Danaher, stopping him in the 14th round. They are fights which rank among the best in the story of British boxing. But that night in Belfast, Tommy Armour battered Boon and stopped him in the fifth round. I was a spectator and can still recall the anguished look on the face of the young Jack Solomons, who was Boon's manager, as he sponged the battered face. My brother John won his bout inside the distance, while among the losers that night was, interestingly, a future world champion, Rinty Monaghan. He was beaten on points by Ike Weir.

By now my fingers had healed and I was back in training. I resumed action in Belfast with a fourth-round win over Jim Josephs whom I had already beaten. My next opponent was more interesting – none other than Jim 'Spider' Kelly. We fought on 5 August 1943, at Brandywell Grounds, Derry.

Spider had won the Irish featherweight title back in 1936 and soon afterwards added the British and Empire titles. He was a veteran of over a hundred professional fights when I climbed into the ring with him and he was also well past his best. But the old champion still had class and he made me work very hard before I earned a ten-round decision. Spider continued boxing right up to 1948. By then his son Billy was ready to take over from him and he went on to emulate his father by winning both the British and Empire featherweight titles in the mid-fifties. Some would argue that, in fairness, Billy also won the European title. But crafty Ray Famechon of France held on to that title in Dublin on a summer's evening in 1955. Most people thought the decision belonged to Kelly. When the verdict was announced there was pandemonium. One fan dumped a bucket of water over promoter Jack Solomons!

I did not go back to my job as a sawyer. Twice I had nearly lost fingers and there was a saying in the trade that you were not fully qualified until you had lost at least one. Friends got me a job as a builder's labourer, digging foundations for an extension of the Veterinary College in Ballsbridge.

I had never previously done such work and it promised a pleasant change. On the first morning, I attacked with enthusiasm, swinging the pick with abandon, until a roar came from behind: "Jaysus, Jimmy, do you want to kill the both of us?" I turned around and immediately saw the problem. Each time I swung the pickaxe over my head, the man behind, Tommy Corr, risked being impaled. Tommy was soon to show me the fundamentals of the building trade. Those were twelve interesting months working at the Veterinary College. I was able to observe much of what was going on, including in the surgeries.

The saddest thing I saw was a beautiful racehorse being put down. It had a tumour on its brain. They did not use a humane killer as it would have damaged the tumour and prevented further study of it. Instead they inserted a hollow needle into the jugular vein and pumped water from a stirrup-pump through the needle. Slowly, ever so slowly, the water replaced the blood, the eyes closed, the head dropped, the front legs folded and the beautiful animal kneeled over, dead. Then they cut off the horse's head and took it away to the laboratory to study the tumour.

I was due for a return bout with Tommy Armour on 9 October 1943. In the run-up to it, I had three inside-the-distance wins. I trained most diligently for that return. John and I were up every morning at six o'clock and running at Sandymount Strand. We trained at Pat Mulcahy's gym in the Palace Cinema where I sparred with Pat, Tommy Upton and Siki O'Neill.

It was six months since my first meeting with Armour in which I had taken a most cruel beating over ten rounds. This time it was a complete contrast, at least to the extent that I wasn't getting hit. For ten rounds I retreated as hooks, swings and uppercuts missed by inches and often by a lot less. All of the time, I was remembering the pain I had endured in the first fight. As the rounds wore on, it dawned on me that, for the first time in my career, I was afraid to have a go. When the bell rang ending the contest I sank wearily on to the corner stool. Naturally, Armour got the decision. But the flesh hadn't been torn off my ribs and my face hadn't been beaten to pulp.

I had just completed my first year as a professional. I'd had nineteen fights, winning seventeen and losing two on points to Ireland's most devastating puncher, Tommy Armour. My brother John was knocked out in the third round by Jim Nugent, his first defeat in the professional ranks. Ruefully rubbing his chin in the dressingroom, he grinned and said to me: "We'll rise again." True enough, he knocked out Nugent a year later.

That was a very severe winter of 1943-1944. By then, Tommy Corr and I were hod carriers on the building site. It was my first experience of that hard graft. The snow came down heavy in December and all work was suspended. In those times you were not paid if the weather prevented work.

So, for a whole month we were unemployed. The dole was just over £1 a week. I was therefore pleased when Bob Gardiner fixed me up to fight Seaman Jim Brown from Co. Antrim on 8 January at the Ulster Stadium. It proved to be quite a fight. In the second round, I landed some good punches to Brown's chin and he took a count of seven. The bell rang. He looked all-in and slumped in his corner. But he came out for the third round. It appeared as if a push would topple him. His hands were held low and his chin exposed. I threw a short right to end it quickly. There was a bright flash in front of my eyes and my head felt as if it had been torn from my shoulders. I hit the canvas with a thud. With difficulty I was on my feet at the count of eight. Then another punch put me down again. Once more I was up at the count of eight. But I was wide open. A right hook exploded on my chin and down I went a third time. Somehow I managed to be up at the count of nine. Brown moved in to finish me. I was entirely at his mercy, but the bell rang.

A spongeful of icy water had me quickly regain my senses. When the bell sounded, I moved quickly from the corner. Brown came on, throwing punches in profusion. I kept retreating and he kept missing. In exasperation, he stopped, dropped his hands and invited me to have a go. It was un-believable. There he stood again, an open target, with chin exposed. Somewhat carefully, I first hit him with a straight left and then crossed a right to land flush on his jaw. He staggered back against the ropes and I followed with a barrage of punches. He slowly sank to the floor and, yet again, the bell intervened. But it was all over in the sixth. He was completely exhausted and the referee stopped it.

It had been a very hard fight and I was looking forward to a week's rest when I received a telegram from Bob Gardiner asking me if I would box Tommy Armour the following Saturday, 15 January, as his opponent had been injured. Three months had passed since my last bout with Tommy. What was there to lose, except my ribs? So I accepted.

Since our last fight, Tommy had beaten Patsy Quinn, Spike McCormack and Freddie Price. They were three of the best men around. Although there wasn't a lot of time, I managed to work out an entirely new approach to Tommy Armour. Instead of staying away and burning myself up trying to avoid his swings and hooks, I decided I would come at him – but from a crouch. So I brought the fight to him all of the time. I beat him to the punch and I beat him round after round. By the fifth round I was so confident that I opened up with both hands and punished him to the head and body as I pinned him on the ropes. I never let his explosive left hand get to work and, throughout the entire fight, I took but two heavy blows. Both were to the body and they rocked me. But I had won every round and I had at last beaten Tommy Armour.

Joe Mirrilson, a Dublin bookmaker, put on a boxing show at Dublin's Theatre Royal on 4 February 1944, with the proceeds going to the Lord Mayor's coal fund. It was quite a bill, topped by Paddy O'Sullivan defending his Éire heavyweight title against Martin Thornton. Another title bout had Corkman Pat Mulcahy and Pat O'Connor in action, while Spike McCormack and I were paired for a £100 purse, winner take all. There was a provision that we both weigh under eleven stone, two pounds. Spike was then a middleweight and I was still a welterweight. There was a forfeit of £20 if one or other was overweight. Jimmy Smith, from Clonmel, was also on the bill – against Terry McStravick, from Belfast. As those who knew it will remember, the Theatre Royal was a huge building – capable of seating more than 4,000 patrons. It was packed that evening and they were well rewarded.

To start with, there was the finest display of courage perhaps ever seen at an Irish venue when Paddy O'Sullivan lost his title to Martin Thornton. Co. Galway man Martin, a professional for seven years, literally cut him to pieces before finally knocking him out in the third round. It was later disclosed that Paddy had been very ill and only went ahead with the contest because he did not want to disappoint the fans. Pat O'Connor won the light-heavyweight championship by outpointing Pat Mulcahay over 15 rounds. It was a wonderful contest. Both Cork lads were accorded a standing ovation from the delighted crowd and nearly ten minutes elapsed before Spike and I could enter the ring for our fight. And what a fight it was. For ten rounds, we belted each other and referee Andy Smith said it was one of the finest bouts he had ever handled. He gave the verdict to Spike by half a point. The fans were once again on their feet cheering us all the way back to the dressing room. The other two bouts were also first class – including Jimmy Smith's win over McStravick. Pat O'Connor, one of the heroes of that night, went to America at the beginning of 1947 and boxed successfully there until the close of 1949.

Eight days after fighting at the Theatre Royal, I was back in Belfast where I beat Freddie Price on points. A few weeks later, I beat Tommy Armour again. This time I really dominated the fight. In the fifth round I had him down and might well have finished it. He fought back bravely in the sixth and I welcomed the bell at the end of that one. On the resumption, Tommy came across the ring like a tornado. I caught him on the chin with a right hook and such was the dual impact that, for a split second, both his feet were off the floor. He sagged into his corner. Now it was my turn. I made every punch count. He sank to his knees. But he was up at the count of nine. I continued pounding. Remembering what I had suffered in my first fight with him, I showed no mercy. The referee eventually intervened. It was now two each, but one of mine was inside the distance.

On 29 April of that year, 1944, I boxed Laurie Buxton, one of the famous brothers from Watford, and it ended in the third round when the referee disqualified him for using the pivot punch. It was a terrible blow, delivered by missing an opponent with a right hand and then bringing the arm back rigidly – striking the jaw. I went down as if I had been pole-axed and was unconscious for a few minutes. My jaw was still sore the next morning and, on the journey home to Dublin,

David Stewart told me of when the pivot punch first made news. It was when French-Canadian George Le Blanche used it in the 32nd round of his bid in August 1889 to take the world middleweight title from Co. Kildare man Jack Dempsey, The Nonpareil. The punch, which nobody had seen before, knocked out Dempsey. But Le Blanche still didn't get the title. He was found to be overweight. Dempsey retained his crown and the pivot punch was there and then declared illegal. Dempsey, whose real name was, of course, John Kelly, eventually lost his title to Bob Fitzsimmons in New Orleans in 1891. Fitzsimmons went on to take the world heavyweight and light-heavyweight titles, in that order. He won the latter from another great Irish-born champion, George Gardiner from Co. Clare. The Nonpareil may well have been the greatest fighter Ireland ever produced. His career was hindered and cut short by ill-health and he died in Oregon in 1895 at the age of thirty-three.

8. A great fiasco

Martin Thornton died in 1983. He had a heart attack while thatching a cottage in his native Spiddal, Co. Galway. He was 68 years of age and had lived life to the full.

The fight between Thornton, then the Irish heavyweight champion, and Bruce Woodcock, who had just become British heavyweight champion, which took place at the Theatre Royal, Dublin, on 24 August 1945, is still much recalled in Ireland. It even remains of media interest. While he was alive, Martin himself, every once in a while, provided a gullible journalist with a new "true version" of what happened that night. Rarely in the history of professional boxing can so insignificant a fight have remained for so long of public interest. No doubt much of it had to do with Martin's own character. He was a most colourful fellow—a hard man in every sense of the word. During his halycon days, he made more news outside the ring than inside it. He also had the old Gaelic gift for story-telling. He was capable of making many of his adventures larger than they ever actually were.

The Dublin bill was put on by Jack Solomons who by the mid-forties was establishing himself as a successful promoter. He showed considerable imagination not so much in matching Thornton and Woodcock but in choosing Dublin as the venue. The fight would have been of only modest interest in Britain. He backed up the main event in Dublin with an excellent supporting bill. It had my brother John challenging Jimmy

Smith for the Irish lightweight title; Joe Boy Collins fighting the former undefeated English amateur Jimmy Webster; Spike McCormack against Paddy Lyons, the North of England middleweight champion; Sean Phillips versus Con Caffrey; and finally, myself paired with the Welsh middleweight champion, Tommy Davis.

But Thornton versus Woodcock was what it was all about that night. In the preceding weeks, the Irish newspapers were full of it. Some were even suggesting that, once Martin had disposed of Woodcock, Joe Louis and the world heavyweight title could be next. Martin trained for the fight at the Mount Street Club in Dublin. I was also training there and acted as his sparring partner.

The Theatre Royal was sold out well in advance and ticket touts made a fortune. All of the preliminary fights were earnestly contested. Then came the big moment. A great hush of expectancy descended on the huge theatre and then the boxers were introduced – Thornton, the heavyweight champion of Ireland, and Woodcock, the heavyweight champion of Great Britain. Thousands of patriotic Irish hearts beat with pride. Furthermore, the fight was broadcast live by Radio Éireann. There can hardly have been an idle wireless in the land and, no doubt, groups of people had gathered around most of them.

Alas, the fight was an utter fiasco. Thornton, who normally began aggressively, came out of his corner like a man already beaten. He covered up and endeavoured to stay out of trouble. Meanwhile, Woodcock began to reach him with straight lefts. Before the round ended, Martin was bleeding from a cut eye. The fight was as good as over in the third round. Thornton, giving up all pretence of trying, stood and stuck out his tongue at Woodcock. The crowd was enraged. To add to it, Thornton then appealed to referee Andy Smythe to stop the fight. He contemptuously told him to box on. Then Thornton's seconds threw in the towel. That was the extent of it. Three weeks later, the Éire Boxing Board of Control suspended Thornton *sine die.*

Martin himself was quite brash about it all. Later that night and the next day he told all who wanted to hear that, prior to the fight, he had insisted in getting in advance from Jack Solomons his £800 purse which he then wagered on Woodcock. As late as February 1981, Martin was regaling readers of the *Sunday Press* with the "real inside story" in which he claimed that he had been paid £4,000 to take a dive. What nonsense!

The key to the whole affair was that, on 19 November 1943, in Manchester, Woodcock, then a youngster on the way up, had destroyed Martin, who was then at his peak, in two rounds. It was virtually a foregone conclusion that Woodcock was going to do so again in Dublin less than two years later. But, such was the publicity and natural Irish enthusiasm for its own champion that no cognizance was taken of the previous meeting between these fighters. However, Martin himself knew that he had little or no chance of beating Woodcock and he did insist on being paid in advance. Some years later, in his book *Solomon Tells All*, Jack Solomons admitted having paid Martin in advance under the threat that if he didn't do so the Co. Galway man would pull out of the fight at virtually the last moment.

What Martin did with the money then is anybody's guess, but we can take it that, if he did get it on Woodcock, it was hardly with shrewd Dublin bookmakers who knew the form. Despite the odium attaching to that fight, Martin Thornton had a fine record. As a professional he knocked out fourteen opponents, won six fights on stoppages, three on disqualifications and two on points. He also, of course, had quite a few losses. Most of his campaigning was done in Britain during the war years, but his reputation was made in Ireland where he hammered any local opponent who came his way. In Ireland he became something of a legend.

But back to the rest of us who fought earnestly that night in Dublin for very modest payment. My brother John deservedly beat Jimmy Smith on points to take the Irish lightweight title. Spike McCormack had a narrow victory over Paddy Lyons, while I beat Tommy Davis. It was a good performance, considering that I was still a welterweight and he the Welsh middleweight champion. But I was again putting on weight and soon would be a middleweight. Standing only five feet, seven inches, I was a small middleweight and this was to tell during my remaining years of paid fighting.

I had a good win over Freddie Price in October in Belfast and was then matched with Spike McCormack for the Irish middleweight title. The bout was set for the Electric Cinema, Dublin on 24 November. I felt great in training until a week before the fight when I went down with gastro-enteritis. I was unable to continue training and lost ten pounds in weight in five days. My doctor advised me to pull out. But promoter Gerald Egan was paying me £100 – the biggest purse to date in my career. Furthermore, there was no chance of Egan getting a suitable substitute. I spent the days before the fight in bed and then went ahead and did my duty.

Despite the loss of weight, I found myself enjoying the fight. When I returned to my corner at the end of the twelfth round, David Stewart was delighted and assured me that I was well ahead on points. Then disaster struck in the thirteenth. Watty Meehan, McCormack's manager, told him that the only way he could win was to stop me. So, Spike came out throwing punches from the start. Foolishly, I joined in and emerged from the mélée with an inch gash over my left eye. Referee Andy Smythe had one look at it and led me to my corner. "I just can't let you continue, Jimmy. The cut is too bad," he said. Afterwards, my doctor told me I was lucky Andy Smythe had acted so promptly. It was a nasty cut, just over the eyelid.

Also on the bill was one Martin Thornton. He stopped Butcher Howell, another heavyweight who contributed much to the colour and excitement of Irish boxing in those days. Only three months had elapsed since Thornton's meeting with Bruce Woodcock. So much for the suspension *sine die*!

But then things moved quickly in those days. Four weeks after getting that badly cut eye, I myself was in action again against Tommy Armour. This time it ended in a draw. We were still even.

At this point, I had no job and a friend, Jack Darby, introduced me to Paddy Brown, the supervisor of the Coras Iompair Éireann depot at Ballsbridge where all tram repairs were carried out. I got a job as a cleaner and I was to spend five happy years with CIE. I met many great characters during those years. Some have now departed this world, but I remember them all with great affection. Paddy Brown was the boss. He never had to be asked for time off when I was boxing. He had great loyalty from his workforce. Those were demanding times, when materials were scarce and improvisation was the order of the day. The tram depot at Ballsbridge gave a great service to Dubliners. There was team loyalty and company loyalty.

I especially remember redheaded Frank Radford who played football for Shelbourne and would surely have won an international cap for Ireland but for the war. He worked at the depot until 1950 when the trams were taken off and replaced by buses. Frank married Joan Byrne, a daughter of Nurse Byrne who brought me into the world. Soon after I came to live in Britain Frank died, still a young man, of a heart attack. But his cheerful smile and the sense of comradeship which he conveyed to all remain vivid with me.

Jimmy Kelly was a veteran nearing retirement when I joined CIE. What a natural entertainer he was – perfect double for Dublin's famous comedian Jimmy O'Dea. Not a day passed without Jimmy delighting us. During dinner-breaks was when he "took the stage". I could go on at great length about these men – Ned O'Toole, the blacksmith at the depot; Andy Moran, his grey hair covered with dust as he polished the brass fittings for the trams; Tommy Jenkins; Paddy Doyle; Robin Lawler; Tommy Hennessy; Dick Ledwidge; Tommy Toal; and Paddy Billane. They were friends and great colleagues. I will always remember the day when Andy Moran turned suddenly to me as I was sweeping around his machine and said: "Jimmy, I have lost a finger." A fitting he was polishing had caught in the revolving spinner and pulled the index finger from his hand. His face turned the colour of his grey hair and he fainted. I caught him before he hit the floor.

My brother John and I decided we would learn to dance. Most of our friends were good ballroom dancers. But since childhood we had been so immersed in boxing that we had never learned. So we went along to Frank Sherwin's School of Dancing in Gardiner Street every Friday evening so as to learn the basics. We paid two shillings and sixpence for an hour's tuition and became proficient in the waltz and the quickstep. The tango was more demanding, but with Frank Sherwin's encouragement we made some progress too with those intricate steps.

The Shelbourne Football Club was running a dance at the Olympic Ballroom and John and I, accompanied by two pals, Peter MacAsey and Jerry Wall, decided to make our dancing debuts that evening. Eddie Downey, of boxing fame, was the ballroom manager and he gave me a warm welcome when I arrived with John and my friends. He asked when I had started dancing. I told him this was my first occasion. He wished me well. I enjoyed myself immensely and danced with a girl named Bridie O'Brien. I asked if I could leave her home and she consented. It was the beginning of a friendship which, two years later, was to result in marriage.

I was nominated to box Spike McCormack for the Irish middleweight crown on 15 June 1945, at Dalymount Park. Our last battle (in which I had got that cut eye) was a crowd-pleaser and we were both, of course, popular Dubliners. So thousands turned up on the night to see the return fight. Once again the promoter was the late Gerald Egan and he put on a good supporting bill. As always, Spike and I gave it all we had. Round after round we battled earnestly. At the end of the fifteenth round referee Andy Smythe called us both to the centre of the ring and raised our hands. It was a draw. The crowd roared in approval.

By now, I had been boxing professionally for three years. I'd had 39 fights – winning 30, drawing two, and losing seven. All of those fights had taken place in Ireland. The war had seen to that. But now the war in Europe was over and new opportunities were about to present themselves. I was in action again three weeks later in Belfast, against one of the greatest characters with whom I ever shared a ring. His name was Jimmy Bray and he was from Bootle. During those eight rounds, I hit him with every punch in the book and he just smiled and belted me back. The packed Ulster Stadium cheered and clapped as we tried and tried again to annihiliate each other. I was exhausted at the end and Jimmy put his arm around my shoulders and said: "A great fight. You did very well." I got the decision, but in my heart I felt it should have been a draw. I told this to Jimmy afterwards in the dressing room. He just smiled. I asked him how on earth he took my best punches without even flinching. He said he had boxed heavyweights and light-heavyweights, none of whom had put him on the floor.

I had my first professional fight outside of Ireland on 8 January 1946 at the Royal Tennis Hall, Stockholm. My opponent was Anton Raadik of Estonia. He had won the European middleweight amateur title in Dublin in 1939. Olle Tanberg of Sweden, who had won the heavyweight title then, topped the bill against Jack Porter of Scotland. Also on the bill was Galwayman Freddie Price who won his fight on points and made a hit with the crowd. I won too, but on a foul. Raddik hit me low in the third round and was instantly disqualified. In those days the jock-strap was a thin piece of aluminium. There was no disputing whether or not the blow was low. It was delivered with such force that the aluminium was badly dented.

In March 1946 Jack Solomons took over Dublin's Theatre Royal once again to put on an excellent bill which had world flyweight champion Jackie Patterson fight Belfast's Eddie "Bunty" Doran in a non-title fight and had me matched with British welter and middleweight champion Ernie Roderick. This, for me, was the big one. I had seen Roderick go the distance with Henry Armstrong for the world welterweight title in London in 1939. Having continued to dominate that division in Britian, Ernie added the British middleweight title in 1945.

I really fought well that night. Roderick was a real craftsman and he had in his corner his brother-in-law, the legendary Nel Tarleton, whose name will always be linked with those of Jimmy Wilde and Jim Driscoll. I was well on top at the half-way stage. Then misfortune struck. That old cut opened over my left eye and Ernie, as the tactics of the game demanded, then concentrated on the injury. By the end of the sixth round, the eye was virtually closed and I could hardly see from it. I would reckon that he probably won the next two rounds. And at that stage it should have been about even. I put all I had into the last two rounds and, despite my handicap, troubled him throughout the ninth round. I won that round well and, at worst, shared the tenth. But it was declared a draw. The crowd demonstrated angrily and I must admit I was very disappointed. A win would have put me in the big time. Still, disappointments soon fade when you are young.

9. Hall of Fame

With the war over and Europe slowly returning to normal, I began to get the big fight opportunities which previously hadn't been available. But by then I was past my peak. It wasn't something which one admitted to oneself or even thought about. There was still a great excitement; I was a natural enthusiast: boxing was my life.

I lost on points over eight rounds to Ginger Sadd of Norwich at Hull on 3 July 1946 and nine days later I boxed the great French middleweight champion Robert Charron at Dalymount Park, Dublin. Shortly before that, Charron had lost to the legendary Marcel Cerdan who was to go on and win the world middleweight title. The Dublin show was promoted by Bill Fuller and word was that Charron was being paid in excess of £2,000. What I know for sure is that my purse was £50 – the same as I had been paid a few months earlier when I drew with British champion Ernie Roderick.

The fight was pretty even for the first seven rounds. Then in the eight he caught me with a terrible left hook to the solar plexus. I was doubled up in agony and he set about finishing me off. I took a barrage of punches to the chin and sank to the canvas. I didn't hear the bell. The next thing I remember was my manager, David Stewart, telling me to keep my hands up. He was sponging me with ice-cold water. Then the bell rang for the ninth round. Charron was all over me. He ripped hooks to the body and then belted me to the head. I went down for a count of nine. Referee Harry Hanly allowed the fight to continue. Another barrage of punches had me down again. But once more I beat the count. I was out on my feet and David Stewart wisely threw in the towel, probably saving me from the first knock-out of my career.

The following January, I was matched with Vince Hawkins in Jersey in the Channel Islands. The previous October, Vince had taken the British middleweight title from Ernie Roderick on a points decision. My brother John was also on the Jersey bill.

Various travel controls which had been introduced during the war were still in operation. I had to go to the British Embassy in Dublin to have my Irish passport stamped for entering Jersey. When I arrived at Dun Laoghaire to catch the mail boat, an official refused to allow me on board. A clerk at the British Embassy had stamped my passport January 1946 instead of January 1947. Needless to say, the boat had gone by the time I had been back to the embassy again to have the matter rectified. We still had time in hand, however, and caught the next boat. There was a terrible storm with mountainous waves. Soon, John and I were violently ill. To add to it, we arrived at Holyhead eight hours behind schedule. From Holyhead, we travelled to Southampton to catch another boat to Jersey. As luck would have it, that too was an appalling crossing with the boat bobbing up and down like a cork. Two wretched human beings eventually crawled ashore on Jersey. And I was about to fight the British middleweight champion! When I saw the superbly fit Vince Hawkins at the weigh-in, I nearly got sick again.

Freddie Mills, the world light-heavyweight champion, was giving an exhibition on the bill. He was accompanied by his manager, Ted Broadribb, who, had the war not intervened in 1939, had been all set to manage my professional career. He greeted me warmly and kindly consented to act as my second. My manager, David Stewart, had been unable to travel to Jersey.

It turned out to be a great fight. Hawkins knocked me down

in the second round with a left hook to the chin. I took a count of eight. In the fourth round, a right hand to the body doubled me in agony and I went through the ropes, tumbling on to the ground. But I scrambled back into the ring before the referee could finish the count. Hawkins came out for the fifth, set to finish it. But I had made a good recovery and hit him with a right hook which, had it landed on the chin, might have ended the contest there and then. As it happened, it hit him on the right eyebrow which split as would a tomato. Now it was my turn to give some stick and for the remainder of the fight he was on the receiving end. The last round had the islanders on their feet cheering us as we tried to annihilate one another. When the bell sounded referee Teddy Waltham held up Hawkins' arm in victory.

That's how it goes!

The following June Dick Turpin beat Hawkins on points in Birmingham to become the first black man to win a British professional title.

By now, I had lost my last four fights – to Ginger Sadd, Robert Charron, Sadd again and Vince Hawkins. But all had been very good fights. The crowds had delighted in them and the press reported most favourably. I may have been losing, but I was still selling tickets. In March 1947 I had my first fight in London. My opponent was Albert Finch, from Croydon, who would soon take the British middleweight title from Dick Turpin. The venue was Seymour Hall. I have in front of me as I write a newspaper cutting. The headline is "Great Rally Wins Finch Verdict Over Ingle". It sums it up correctly. I was well ahead on points after five rounds. But Albert came back strongly and probably did enough in the last two rounds to justify referee Teddy Waltham's giving him the verdict.

In 1980 Albert visited me at my home in Luton and we had a long chat during which he remarked: "Jimmy, I'm glad to see you still have all your marbles." We both knew that lots of fellows who had gone through the boxing mill in those days weren't so lucky.

On 2 May 1947, Spike McCormack was to defend his Irish middleweight title against Bert Hyland at Dublin's Tolka Park. A few days before the fight, Hyland was injured and promoter Gerald Egan pleaded with me to take his place. I had just begun training to fight Jack Johnson, of British Guiana, in Guernsey in the Channel Islands the following month. I wasn't ready to engage in a fifteen-round title fight. Eventually, a compromise was reached. It would be a ten-round affair.

I was getting married in July and I asked Bridie if she would like to go to the show; she had never seen me box before and was very nervous in case I might get hurt. It was a great battle, as were all my tangles with the colourful Spike, and I won on points. I asked Bridie if she had enjoyed it. She had not seen a single round; being too afraid to look. It was the first and last time she ever came to a fight.

There was little time to celebrate my victory over Spike and in Guernsey I was knocked out for the first time in my entire boxing career. In the third round, Johnson, who stood six feet, swung a right hook which caught me in the groin. I was paralysed as referee Teddy Waltham counted me out. It was fully five minutes before I could leave the ring. A large section of the crowd booed Johnson believing, correctly, that he had hit me low. He responded with a derisive gesture which further aggravated the crowd. But the referee's decision was final. Afterwards, I received a letter from the promoter assuring me that it was a low punch and asking me to box Randolph Turpin at the Butts Stadium, Coventry, on 9 September.

Bridie and I were married in the Pro-Cathedral in Marlborough Street on 21 July 1947, my twenty-sixth birthday. John was my best man and Lilly Brennan, a first cousin of Bridie's, was bridesmaid. There were a lot of children waiting outside the church and, as was the usual practice, I threw a handful of coins into their midst and it was bedlam as they jostled and pushed each other. We spent our honeymoon in Bundoran, a beautiful spot in Donegal, where we enjoyed lovely weather. After a week we returned to Dublin, to our

Wedding day: *John Ingle, best man; Jimmy; Bridie; Bridie's cousin and brides-maid, Lillie Brennan.*

new home in Stanford Green in Walkinstown, and I began to prepare for my fight with Turpin.

Randolph Turpin was a magnificent boxing machine. He had a brilliant amateur career and was now en route to the British and world middleweight titles. For this fight I was being paid £200 – by far the biggest purse of my boxing career. I trained most diligently. I was up at six o'clock each morning and, accompanied by Paddy Brennan on his bicycle, I ran to Tallaght and back, approximately ten miles. A bath and a rub-down followed before going back to bed for a couple of hours. I had plenty of time because the tram depot at Ballsbridge, where I worked, had closed down. I had been transferred to Spa Road, Inchicore. Soon afterwards we had been called out on strike. So there was all the time I needed for training. I had two splendid sparring partners: Mick McKeown and Willie Duggan. They were, of course, outstanding Irish amateur champions.

No less than 10,000 people packed the Butts Stadium, Coventry, that night. Virtually all were, of course, Turpin fans. The reception he received when introduced from the ring lasted for at least a minute – the crowd standing, clapping and cheering. Randolph was their hero and deservedly so. The fight lasted three rounds. Afterwards I could recall only the first minute. A right-hand punch exploded on my chin and for the remainder of the bout I boxed only from instinct. Later David Stewart told me I was down for three counts of nine in every round and that the referee had stopped it at the end of round three.

Having won all the glory which professional boxing could offer, as well as huge financial rewards, Randolph Turpin had a tragic life. It's all in Jack Birtley's biography, *The Tragedy of Randolph Turpin*.

The strike at CIE went on for five months and the £200 which I earned against Turpin came in very useful as our strike pay was only £2 a week. During the strike, it began to dawn on me that I wasn't hearing from promoters. The year ended without a single fight offer. I felt that I didn't deserve that. I'd had 51 professional fights during the previous five years and had boxed not alone the best men in the islands but also some of the best in Europe. I had won 34 fights, drawn three, and lost fourteen. I was still only 26 years of age. Was my career over? I continued training at the Crumlin Boxing Club. Eventually the strike at CIE ended. It achieved an extra two pence an hour (less than a present-day penny). It brought our wages up to £5.10s for a 47-hour week.

January, February and March passed and I still hadn't received a single fight offer. Bridie was expecting our first child in August. The baby was born on 17 August 1948 and we named him Charles David after my father and my manager. I then had a letter from Belfast promoter Bob Gardiner asking if I would fight in Liverpool on 28 October. I was delighted to accept. My opponent was Billy Jackson from Jamaica. He was disqualified in the fifth round for butting. I caught the boat from Liverpool to Belfast and boxed there two nights later, beating Frank Boylan on points. The *Belfast Telegraph* gave me a good write-up saying that, after an absence of twelve months from the ring, I had displayed all of my old craft and had scored a decisive win.

Next came a fight in Glasgow – at Grove Stadium where, in the past, many of Scotland's great champions had performed. I received a wonderful reception from the fans when the MC announcd that it was my first engagement in the city. My opponent was Jack Brown, from Doncaster, and it was a terrific fight for three rounds with Jack refusing to take a backward step. We really belted one another and he failed to come out for the fourth round having damaged his right arm by landing on my head a terrific punch which was aimed at my chin.

As a result of that good win, promoter Johnny McMillan invited me back to Glasgow on 1 January 1949, to box Scottish middleweight title contender Billy Stevens. We were top of the bill. That afternoon, before the fight, I was invited to a

Celtic-Rangers match. It was a wonderful exhibition of football between two of the best clubs in the business which Celtic won. That night, after a most entertaining fight, Billy Stevens was given the verdict. But it must have been close.

My trainer, David Stewart, who had guided my career since my early teens, soon afterwards reached his 70th birthday. He felt he could no longer act as my manager and trainer because the strain of travelling was too much for him. I saw David for the last time in August 1970, when Bridie and our family were holidaying in Dublin. He lived until the age of 86 and I will always remember him with great affection. We never had a written contract and we never needed one.

Jim Callaghan from Belfast then became my manager, again on no more than a handshake. He looked after my interests for the remainder of my career.

The evening of 23 June 1949 remains fresh in my memory. I was matched with Bert Hyland to decide the challenger for Spike McCormack's middleweight title. Once again the venue was Dalymount Park and the promoter Gerald Egan. Gerald had worked hard to make it a big occasion. He had brought over American Lee Savold, who was a top contender for the world heavyweight title, to box an exhibition with the Irish heavyweight champion, Gerry Kilcullen, and Don Mogard. Mogard's stablemate, Solly Cantor, was paired with Paddy Dowdall. There were also quite a few other good fights on the bill, but somehow the show didn't catch the public's imagination. On turning up at Dalymount, Savold's manager Billy Daly, remarked: "Gee, everybody is here except the crowd."

It was still a great night's boxing. Paddy Dowdall showed much of his old craft against Solly Cantor. The verdict was a draw, but most of us felt that Paddy should have got the decision. I too got a bad decision, losing on points to Bert Hyland. That wasn't just my view. The crowd greeted the verdict with prolonged booing.

I then had a return bout, in the Isle of Man, with Billy Stevens who had beaten me on points the previous January in

Glasgow. It was an open-air show in Douglas and attracted a crowd of more than 3,000. We gave them good value for money and I won on points. Three months later we fought again in Belfast and once more I got the verdict.

I was by now being regularly troubled by that scar over my left eye which first opened against Spike McCormack in November 1945. It had since opened on a number of occasions and my brother John then burst it open during a sparring session. When stitching it again, Dr. Hannigan advised me to think hard about continuing boxing. "You have been fighting for seventeen years, both amateur and professional, and that's a long time," he said. Bridie was expecting our second child in December. I told her what Dr. Hannigan had said and she indicated that she would be very relieved if I retired.

Before we had time to think any more about it, a telegram arrived from Bob Gardiner offering me £75 to substitute for Tommy Armour who, as a result of an injury, was forced to pull out of a fight with Jackie Wilson. I immediately accepted. After all, it represented three months' wages for half an hour's boxing. But, alas, the eye-wound opened at the end of the third round. The blood poured and after the referee had examined the eye during the break, he stopped the fight.

Strangely enough, the eye healed quickly and the stitches were out in a week. I resumed training at the Crumlin Boxing Club and, for the first time ever, donned headgear while sparring with Mick McKeown and Willie Duggan. On 5 December I again fought Albert Finch, this time at Leeds Town Hall, for a purse of £75 with all expenses paid. I did well for the first four rounds. Then I walked into a right-hand punch which put me on the floor for a count of nine. On getting up, a welter of hooks and swings had me on the floor again. I staggered as I attempted to rise and the referee immediately stopped the fight.

Our second son was born on Christmas Eve. We christened him Noel. The coach-builders at CIE depot at the Spa Road, Inchicore, made a beautiful horse and cart as a Christmas present for our first son, Charles.

I had my last fight on 13 June 1950, against Alex Buxton at Watford Town Hall. He was later to be British light-heavyweight champion. The fight had hardly begun before a right-hand punch landed on my bad eye, and in an instant I had double vision. There were two Buxtons in the ring and two sets of gloves belting me. The referee quickly intervened and stopped the fight. When I returned home, I told Bridie that I would never box again. I'd had a good run.

A spell of unemployment followed. My many visits to Britain during the preceding years had made me develop a liking for the country and so it was that, with prospects bleak in Dublin, Bridie and I and family crossed the Irish Sea. We settled in Luton. We have been happy here and have raised a fine family, and in 1960 I had the pleasure of being involved with Michael Hawes, who hails from Co. Clare, in forming the Luton Irish Boxing Club.

In 1983, when the *Irish Post* announced its annual sports awards, I was chosen for the "Hall of Fame". A few months later, The *Irish Post* and B & I hosted a delightful evening at the National Golf Centre in Wishaw, Sutton Coldfield. There were lots of other award recipients, among them Alex "Hurricane" Higgins and golfing star John O'Leary. My award was a bronze replica of Oliver Sheppard's splendid statue of Cuchulainn in Dublin's GPO. Bridie, as well as our sons Noel and Jimmy Jnr. and our daughter Joan, accompanied me to the awards evening. We all enjoyed it very much. It was nice to be remembered.

Jimmy Ingle is presented with the Hall of Fame award by Jim Kennedy of B & I, May 1983.

Jimmy Ingle's Professional Record

Key: W=won; L=lost; D=drew; Disq.=disqualified; K.O.=knock-out; R.s.f.=referee stopped fight; Rtd=retired.

1942

9 Oct	Chuck Flannigan	W R.s.f. 2	Dublin
17 Oct	Jim Hamilton	W Pts 8	Belfast
23 Oct	Pat Kelly	W K.O. 2	Dublin
31 Oct	Tommy Williams	W R.s.f. 5	Belfast
21 Nov	Jim Doran	W R.s.f. 6	Belfast
27 Nov	Patsy Quinn	W Pts 8	Dublin
5 Dec	Andy McLoughlin	W Rtd 4	Belfast
11 Dec	Patsy Quinn	W Pts 8	Belfast
19 Dec	Patsy Quinn	W Pts 8	Belfast

1943

6 Feb	Jim Josephs	W Rtd 6	Belfast
27 Feb	Jim Hamilton	W Rtd 6	Belfast
20 Mar	Tommy Armour	L Pts 10	Belfast
10 Apr	Jack Clancy	W Pts 8	Belfast
1 May	Jack Clancy	W Pts 8	Belfast
3 Aug	Jim Spider Kelly	W Pts 8	Derry
27 Aug	Jim Doran	W Rtd 3	Dublin
18 Sept	Ivan Williams	W Rtd 3	Belfast
25 Sept	Matt Locke	W Rtd 5	Belfast
9 Oct	Tommy Armour	L Pts 10	Belfast

1944

5 Jan	Seaman Jim Brown	W Rtd 6	Belfast
15 Jan	Tommy Armour	W Pts 8	Belfast
4 Feb	Spike McCormack	L Pts 10	Belfast
12 Feb	Freddie Price	L Pts 8	Belfast
1 Apr	Tommy Armour	W Rtd 7	Belfast
29 Apr	Laurie Buxton	W Disq. 3	Belfast
13 May	Matt Locke	W Pts 8	Belfast
16 June	Jack Clancy	W R.s.f. 8	Dublin
14 July	Matt Locke	W K.O. 4	Dublin
18 Aug	Spike McCormack	L Pts 10	Dublin
16 Sept	Jack Clancy	W R.s.f. 9	Dublin
11 Oct	Pat Mulcahy	W Pts 10	Derry
28 Oct	Freddie Price	W Pts 8	Belfast
24 Nov	Spike McCormack	L R.s.f. 13	Dublin
23 Dec	Tommy Armour	D 10	Belfast

1945

9 Feb	Patsy Quinn	W Rtd 2	Dublin
9 Mar	Tommy Armour	W Rtd 5	Dublin
28 Apr	Freddie Price	L Pts 8	Belfast
15 June	Spike McCormack	D 15	Dublin
24 Aug	Tommy Davis	W Pts 10	Dublin
18 Sept	Jimmy Bray	W Pts 10	Belfast
26 Dec	Taffy Williams	W Rtd 6	Belfast

1946

8 Jan	Anton Raadik	W Disq. 3	Stockholm
8 Mar	Ernie Roderick	D 8	Dublin
3 July	Ginger Sadd	L Pts 8	Hull
12 July	Robert Charron	L Rtd 9	Dublin
24 Sept	Ginger Sadd	L Pts 8	Belfast

1947

11 Jan	Vince Hawkins	L Pts 8	Jersey
11 Mar	Albert Finch	L Pts 8	London
2 May	Spike McCormack	W Pts 10	Dublin
8 June	Jack Johnson	L K.O. 3	Guernsey
9 Sept	Randolph Turpin	L R.s.f. 3	Coventry

1948

8 June	Jack Brown	W Rtd 3	Glasgow
28 Oct	Bill Jackson	W Disq. 6	Liverpool
30 Oct	Frank Boylan	W Pts 8	Belfast

1949

1 Jan	Billy Stevens	L Pts 8	Glasgow
1 Mar	Bill Jackson	L Pts 8	Edinburgh
23 June	Bert Hyland	L Pts 10	Dublin
21 July	Billy Stevens	L Pts 8	Glasgow
1 Oct	Billy Stevens	W Pts 8	Douglas
19 Nov	Jackie Wilson	L R.s.f. 2	Belfast
5 Dec	Albert Finch	L R.s.f. 5	Leeds

1950

| 21 Mar | Billy Carroll | W Pts 8 | Edinburgh |
| 13 June | Alex Buxton | L R.s.f. 1 | Watford |

Summary
Won 40; drew 3; lost 20.

New From Brandon

The Fighting Irish: A History of Irish Boxing

by Patrick Myler

Jack Dempsey, Dan Donnelly, Jack Doyle, Barry McGuigan, Rinty Monaghan, John L. Sullivan and Gene Tunney: the names span the years from the bare knuckle days to the present. But these are only a small selection of the Irish names that have been famous in one generation or another for their boxing skills.

The facts are gathered in this book as never before, the most important bouts are described, the records of individual fighters assessed. There are fascinating insights, too, into the boxing world and into the social circumstances of the Irish in Britain and the United States.

Patrick Myler is admirably qualified to write the definitive study of the Irish contribution to boxing. He is the author of *Regency Rogue*, a biography of Dan Donnelly; he is a life-long boxing enthusiast who has worked as a news and sports reporter in England; he has contributed to *Boxing Illustrated* and he is the Irish correspondent of *Boxing News*.

Fully illustrated, hardback; September 1985

Also published by Brandon

John B. Keane: Man of the Triple Name

"Anybody who enjoys old-style storytelling at its best should reach for *Man of the Triple Name*." – *Irish Post*
"This lyrical, most human and highly humorous book." – Benedict Kiely, *The Irish Times*
"Hilarious social history." – *Boston Irish News*
"Hugely enjoyable." – *In Dublin*
Hardback and paperback

Paddy Lysaght: An Irish Literary Quiz Book

Illustrated by Tom Mathews
"Both amusing and interesting . . . not only does it test the knowledge of the reader but it reminds of the value of certain books and if you're lucky enough to have them available will send you straight back to reading them again . . . Irresistible."
– Frank Delaney, *Sunday Press*
"A delight and a storehouse of information." – *Boston Irish News*
"A must for the up-market quiz enthusiast." – *Andersonstown News*
"Delightful . . . tantalising and amusing . . . an ideal volume for a long train journey. At the end one knows a lot more about Irish literature." – *Irish Post*
Paperback

Fr. McDyer of Glencolumbkille: An Autobiography

"Not since Patrick Kavanagh's *The Green Fool* have I read an Irish autobiography which is so true, so real, so riven with earth-born loving, and working and dancing and praying." – *Cork Examiner*
"Fr McDyer's message still rings loud and clear." – *Irish Post*
Hardback and paperback